PLAYING THE RACES

"Playing the Races," *Life* 34 (November 1899): 407.

HENRY B. WONHAM

PLAYING | THE RACES

Ethnic Caricature and American Literary Realism

OXFORD

UNIVERSITY PRESS

2004

OXFORD
UNIVERSITY PRESS

Oxford   New York
Auckland   Bangkok   Buenos Aires   Cape Town   Chennai
Dar es Salaam   Delhi   Hong Kong   Istanbul   Karachi   Kolkata
Kuala Lumpur   Madrid   Melbourne   Mexico City   Mumbai   Nairobi
São Paulo   Shanghai   Taipei   Tokyo   Toronto

Published by Oxford University Press, Inc.
198 Madison Avenue, New York, New York, 10016

www.oup.com

Oxford is a registered trademark of Oxford University Press

Library of Congress Cataloging-in-Publication Data
Wonham, Henry B., 1960–
Playing the races : ethnic caricature and American literary realism/
Henry B. Wonham.
p. cm.
Includes bibliographical references and index.
ISBN 0-19-516194-7
1. American fiction—19th century—History and criticism. 2. Race in
literature. 3. Caricatures and cartoons—United States—History—19th
century. 4. United States—Ethnic relations—History—19th century.
5 United States—Race relations—History—19th century. 6. Stereotype
(Psychology) in litaerature. 7. Ethnicity in literature. 8. Realism in
literature. I. Title
PS374.R32W66 2004
813'.309355—dc21   2003012834

9 8 7 6 5 4 3 2 1

Printed in the United States of America
on acid-free paper

For

Walker Lincoln Wonham

and in memory of

Mary Fronheiser Quarles

ACKNOWLEDGMENTS

Many of the people I wish to thank in these acknowledgments will have no idea that they contributed substantively to my work on this book, and yet their collective insight and example have helped to make *Playing the Races* possible. I owe particular gratitude to my colleagues at the University of Oregon, who have provided support and encouragement for this project in more ways than I have room to mention here. The most tangible expressions of support, often in the form of candid criticism, have come from Karen Ford, Shari Huhndorf, Richard Stein, Glen Love, John Gage, Paul Peppis, and Nic Witschi, all of whom improved the manuscript with their thoughtful advice. It has also been my good fortune to receive guidance from many of the individuals I most respect in the field of American literary studies, including Brook Thomas, Werner Sollors, Gary Scharnhorst, Michael North, Gerd Hurm, John Crowley, and Harold Kolb. My colleagues in Freiburg and at the Charles University in Prague gratified me with their interest in my work during two extraordinarily stimulating terms abroad.

In addition to the encouragement of these and many other individuals, I have benefited from the resourcefulness and technical expertise of librarians at the University of Oregon's Knight Library and the Schomburg Center for Research in Black Culture. The Oregon Center for the Humanities provided a term off and office space for writing and research in the early stages of composition, for which I am very grateful. Portions of the introduction and of chapters two and three were first published in academic journals, and I would like to thank the editors of *American Literature, American Literary*

Realism, and *The Henry James Review* for their useful input. Elissa Morris, Jeremy Lewis, and the editorial staff at Oxford University Press have been models of professionalism in their production of the manuscript.

Finally, I would like to thank my wife Connie for her generosity, support, and unlimited energy. This book is affectionately dedicated to two of the most important people in our lives, Walker Lincoln Wonham, whose birth two years ago reminded us of what we value most, and Mary Fronheiser Quarles, who did not live to see *Playing the Races* in print, but who remains in loving memory my ideal of an educated reader.

CONTENTS

PLAYING THE RACES

INTRODUCTION

The Age of Caricature,
the Age of Realism

Shortly after the Civil War, some of America's most talented painters traveled to the South to examine conditions facing the recently emancipated freedmen. Motivated largely by sympathy for the plight of African Americans, artists such as Winslow Homer and Thomas Eakins applied the latest "realist" techniques to an unprecedented series of portraits and genre paintings of Southern life in the postwar era. The political content of their images often spoke with blunt candor about the significance of Southern race policy, as in Homer's celebrated "Gulf Stream," in which a solitary black fisherman lies prone and exhausted after a tropical storm, clinging to the deck of his foundering vessel, as sharks and menacing waves descend upon him. African Americans had often been depicted in comic imagery of the period as the inevitable victims of natural and political forces beyond their control, but the unaffected dignity and calm reserve of Homer's muscular black subject marked a new direction in the graphic interpretation of African-American character and identity.[1] Critics were quick to appreciate the humanizing power of Homer's realism, which Alain Locke credited with having initiated "the artistic emancipation of the Negro subject in American art."[2]

Although raised by Northern Democrats who opposed the Union cause, Eakins was similarly committed to the individualized treatment of African-American subjects. His "Negro Boy Dancing" deploys minstrelsy's standard clichés, the banjo and top hat, as elements in a complex image of human struggle and aspiration (figure I.1). According to Sydney Kaplan, the somber dancing lesson challenges "the slavophile iconography of banjo, grin, and jig" by reveal-

ing the intense concentration and joyless labor behind the stereotype of the shuffling darky.[3] With thoughtful and exacting expressions, the two seasoned performers fix their gaze upon the neophyte,
whose strained efforts provide an impression of real conditions obscured by the burnt cork mask of blackface performance. As in "Gulf
Stream," realism's attention to individual detail betrays the fiction of
ethnic stereotype, enabling the "artistic emancipation" of the ethnic
subject in American art.

Alain Locke was not alone in linking the political significance of
realism to the larger projects of emancipation for blacks and equal
rights for all Americans. "What American artist has not caricatured
us?," asked an incredulous group of black suffrage activists in 1860,
calling attention to the relationship between constitutional disfran-
chisement and a long tradition of dehumanizing imagery employed
ostensibly to represent African-American life.[4] Caricatures and
stereotypes of ethnic subjects, as Alice Walker has explained, "were
really intended as prisons. Prisons without the traditional bars, but
prisons of image."[5] Realism, as the representational antithesis to
mere caricature, according to this argument, performs the work of

FIGURE 1.1. Thomas Eakins, "Negro Boy Dancing," 1878. The
Metropolitan Museum of Art, New York.

liberation, disentangling the human individual from the distorting grip of ethnic typology. Major late nineteenth-century periodicals, such as *Century* and the *Atlantic Monthly,* embraced this critical formula as a matter of editorial policy, contrasting the liberating force of realism to the conceptual imprisonment of caricature in countless essays and reviews. *Harper's Monthly* joined the chorus in its review of the work of William Sidney Mount, another renowned interpreter of African-American character, and, according to *Harper's,* "the only artist among us who can delineate God's image carved in ebony."6 Demonstrating a profound fidelity to nature, Mount's portrait of a young black gambler in "The Lucky Throw" bears the "humanizing" touch of a "true work of art," not to be confused with "the vulgar and brutal caricatures of the negro which abound" elsewhere in the periodical press.

From his editorial posts at the *Atlantic Monthly* and later *Harper's,* William Dean Howells defended realism in precisely these terms, touting the democratic impulse of realist imagery as a counterforce to romanticism's "pride of caste," which is "averse to the mass of men" and "consents to know them only in some conventionalized and artificial guise."7 Richard Watson Gilder of *Century* was equally confident that a realist aesthetic, once embraced by the public, would perform the vital political function of "suturing," in Kenneth Warren's words, "the wounds that disfigured postbellum society."8 For Alain Locke and others, this seemingly natural conflation of politics and aesthetics pointed unambiguously toward social progress for African Americans. In "American Literary Tradition and the Negro," he argued that realism had loosened "the double grip of social prejudice and moral Victorianism" upon the American imagination, replacing "stock Negro stereotypes" with something approaching an authentic representation of African-American life.9 Another essay, "The Saving Grace of Realism," praised "the simple, unaffected dignity of sympathetic and often poetic realism and the sobriety of the artist who loves and respects his subject-matter."10 A "sound and understanding" realist aesthetic, according to Locke, would revive American interest in the unfinished business of Reconstruction, breeding sympathy, if not "love and respect," for African Americans.

More recent writers have established the link between realist aesthetics and the politics of emancipation as something approaching a literary-critical doctrine. In one of the most influential twentieth-century accounts of Western literary tradition, Erich Auerbach defended the use of seemingly "random moments" in realist practice, explaining that "the more numerous, varied, and simple the people are who appear as subjects of such random moments, the more effectively must what they have in common shine forth."[11] For both Auerbach and Alain Locke, literary realism's democratizing impulse opened channels of sympathy to all people, including the members of groups systematically misrepresented in the elitist art of the dominant culture. Writing in *Century* magazine, Thomas Sergeant Perry summarized the case for realism as a catalyst for progressive social change: "After all, what can realism produce but the downfall of conventionality? Just as the scientific spirit digs the ground from beneath superstition, so does its fellow-worker, realism, tend to prick the bubble of abstract types. Realism is the tool of the democratic spirit, the modern spirit by which the truth is elicited."[12]

Perry's compelling metaphors draw a stark theoretical picture of the relationship between the humanizing truth of realism and the dehumanizing illusion of ethnic caricature, which might be described as the toxic gas that inflates "the bubble of abstract types." Yet this clear distinction tends to collapse in the messy variety of actual late nineteenth-century images and the responses they elicited from their audiences. Consider, for example, the case of William Sidney Mount, whose "The Lucky Throw" impressed *Harper's* as a "true work of art," unlike the "brutal caricatures" that typically served to represent ethnic variety throughout the era (figure I.2). Leaving aside the fact that this painting plays directly upon several aspects of a prevailing stereotype (the notion that African Americans possess unlimited appetites for gambling and poultry), it seems doubtful that Mount conceived of his representational technique as a "tool of the democratic spirit."[13] An outspoken opponent of Reconstruction, he worked assiduously in the political and aesthetic spheres to ensure that "the defunct nigger" would remain "politically dead."[14] Among his most memorable contributions to the national debate over Reconstruction was a painting titled "A Rooster Standing upon a Dead Negro, or The Break of Day," which depicted, according to Mount's analysis, "the Radical Republican Rooster trying to make more capital out of the negro[,] who is about used up for their purpose. . . . The African needs rest."[15]

My point is not that *Harper's* erred in labeling Mount a realist, nor should his retrograde politics compel us to call him instead a caricaturist. Rather, I wish to suggest that politics and aesthetics are more complexly related in the literary and graphic record of American realism than the critical polemics of Howells's time and our own

FIGURE 1.2. Jean-Baptiste Adolphe LaFosse (lithograph reproduction of the painting, now lost, by William Sidney Mount), "The Lucky Throw or Raffling for a Goose," 1851. The Museums at Stony Brook, New York.

would imply. Indeed, Mount's African-American images manage to be distinctly lifelike and perfectly stereotypical at the same time, a paradox that must cast suspicion on the simple linkage of realism and progressive social change. That linkage is similarly tested in many of Homer's paintings of Southern life, which also raise difficult questions about realism's presumed antipathy to ethnic "prisons of image." Homer's profound sense of the humanity of his black subjects is unquestionable, but paintings such as "The Watermelon Boys" and "Dressing for the Carnival" participate just as unquestionably in the period's vibrant discourse of ethnic caricature. Moreover, the irony that underlies Homer's compositions on such hackneyed themes as watermelon stealing and black dandyism did nothing to "prick the bubble of abstract types" in the minds of his admirers, who praised Homer's accurate representation of "darkey women" and "pickaninnies," including his adorable representation of "little darkies eating their watermelon."[16]

It is tempting either to dismiss such comments as the racist cant of a benighted critical sensibility, or—as has been more fashionable in recent years—to accuse artists such as Homer of deep-seated, perhaps even unconscious, complicity with the conservative agenda of a dominant culture willing to pay little more than lip service to the idea of social justice. In the chapters that follow, I propose to resist both of these reactions in order to explore a third possibility, namely that ethnic caricature performs an integral function *within* the political and aesthetic program of American realism. What shall we make of the fact that Winslow Homer required a watermelon patch to represent what many critics considered an image of "the negro . . . as he really is"?[17] Is it a coincidence that so many of the artists and writers who aligned themselves with Howells's democratic aesthetic, including Howells himself, relied heavily on the stock conventions of ethnic caricature? Critics have often dismissed such lapses in realist practice as blind spots, vestiges of a genteel social consciousness that failed to keep pace with realism's avowed democratic aspirations. Such explanations are useful to a point, but they overlook the fact that the age of realism in American art and letters is simultaneously the great age of ethnic caricature. These two aesthetic programs, one committed to representation of the fully humanized individual, the other invested in broad ethnic abstractions, operate less as antithetical choices than as complementary impulses, both of which receive full play within the period's most demanding literary and graphic works. The era Howells claimed for realism in American art and literature was in fact characterized as much by the highly wrought figures of Huck Finn, Silas Lapham, and Lily Bart as it was by Paddy and Bridget, Hockheimer and Rebecca, and Rastus and Chloe, conventional names for the comic types that vied for magazine space in friendly competition with the latest realist fiction. The intriguing proximity of such singular characters and such generic types within the pages of America's major periodicals—indeed the seemingly anomalous presence of ethnic abstractions within works by Mark Twain, Howells, Edith Wharton, and others—hints at realism's vexed and complicated relationship with the caricatured ethnic images that played such a central role in late nineteenth-century American thinking about race, identity, and national culture. My hope is that *Playing the Races* will cast some light on that relationship and on the rich literary discourse conceived at the intersection of the realist and the caricatured image.

Of course, a longstanding critical orthodoxy firmly distinguishes between realism, which "consist[s] in the exactest copying of nature," according to Henry Fielding, and "the Caricatura," whose aim is "to exhibit monsters, not men."[18] Caricature in painting, for Fielding, corresponded to the excesses of literary burlesque, "where our delight, if we examine it, arises from the surprising absurdity, as in appropriating the manners of the highest to the lowest, or *e converso.*" Hogarth similarly insisted upon a clear distinction between "character" and "caricatura," aligning his satires of London social life with the former, against the example of Annibale Carracci, Pier Leone Ghezzi, and other innovators of modern caricature in sixteenth- and seventeenth-century Italy.[19]

Howells picked up this thread of argument in "Criticism and Fiction" by denouncing Dickens and Thackeray as mere caricaturists, writers who shared Balzac's appetite for "the touch of exaggeration which typifies," in contrast to the American realist, who always rejects type in favor of character and individuality.[20] Howells insisted that realism's unique commitment to character reflected the aesthetic temperament of a democratic people, for whom the generality of type was "one of the last refuges of the aristocratic spirit" in literature.[21] Whereas caricature annihilated the individuality of the subject, exaggerating facial or bodily characteristics to reveal the individual as nothing but an expression of abstract tendencies, American realism worked to extend the authority of the self in an atmosphere of increasing uncertainty. Silas Lapham must recover himself after dissipating encounters with the modern consumer marketplace; Huckleberry Finn must attend to a voice "away inside" in order to appreciate his predicament in terms other than those offered by a corrupt society.[22] The American realist novel constantly enacts some version of this morality play, in which the self is threatened, compromised, and problematically reaffirmed as the legitimate arbiter of human experience. Taking his cue from Howells, Joel Chandler Harris in 1892 articulated what had become by then a critical truism: "neither fictive nor illustrative art has any business with types. It must address itself to life, to the essence of life, which is character, which is individuality. Missing these it misses its true function."[23]

According to this logic, the art of caricature is ethically and aesthetically incompatible with American realism, as Howells insisted, and yet in practice these purportedly antithetical categories of representation remain intimately related, as a glance through Harris's Uncle Remus collections will confirm beyond a doubt. One reason for this curious overlap of representational practices may be that, for all their theoretical antipathy, realism and caricature pursue strikingly similar aesthetic aims. Indeed both programs understand their function in terms of "penetration" and "exposure," and both claim a unique capacity to lay bare the "essence" of the human subject. Annibale Carracci, who gave his name to the art of caricature, compared his practice to that of the classical artist, explaining that "one may strive to visualize the perfect form and to realize it in his work, the other to grasp the perfect deformity, and thus reveal the very essence of a personality. A good caricature, like every work of art, is more true to life than reality itself."[24] Ernst Gombrich, one of very few theorists to take the art of caricature seriously, concurred that the mimetic artist and the caricaturist pursue "corresponding" aims. Whereas the painter employs traditional portraiture "to reveal the character, the essence of the man," his counterpart accentuates the subject's deformity, "thus penetrating through the mere outward appearance to the inner being in all its littleness or ugliness."[25]

In addition to sharing a set of conceptual objectives, the realist and the caricaturist employ the same metaphors to describe their aesthetic processes. Howells denied any association with what he considered the decadent art of Flaubert and the primitivism of Balzac, but he followed the great French realists in comparing literary representation to a scientific enterprise. Like a physician, Howells's favorite analogue for his own vocation, the realist works to dispel the mists of fantasy and superstition that obscure the sources of health and disease, comedy and tragedy, opening to view the human subject in its most essential form. Howells was apparently taken at his word, for he and Henry James were lampooned in the popular press as heartless surgeons, motivated by a perverse academic passion to analyze the human organism. (figure I.3)

An 1899 essay on caricature in *Littel's Living Age* suggests that contemporary scholarship recognized little difference between the analytical approach of scientific realism and that of journalistic caricature. Noting that recent efforts in political cartooning aim "not so much to divert by sarcasm as to impress by truth," critic Robert de la Sizeranne observed that the modern caricaturist, much like the modern writer, possesses "something . . . both of the detective and of the surgeon. He should have Roentgen rays in his eyes to discern, as he does, under a mass of flesh and of garments, the special band in the gearing which determines an attitude."[26] De la Sizeranne concluded his analysis with an observation that would have troubled Howells, but that underscores a perverse symmetry between the late nineteenth-century's two dominant representational modes: "Caricature now so closely approaches the exact observation of life that it is difficult to draw the line between the caricaturist and the 'modernist' in art."[27]

FIGURE I.3. "The Modern Novel," *Life* 20 (May 1886).

If the Howellsian artist can usefully be understood as a kind of physician of the soul, as Howells and many of his contemporaries proposed, then his specialty was the science of phrenology, for instead of a scalpel or a Roentgen ray, the realist employs observation and interpretation to make the interior self legible. In fact, the enterprise of American literary realism hinged on the artist's confidence that the essential self—"the essence of the man," in Gombrich's words—can be coherently and reliable interpreted through acts of mimetic representation, a confidence not unlike that of the phrenologist, who claims that an individual's character and destiny are expressed in the features of the face and head. Miles Orvell has provided a rich understanding of late nineteenth-century American culture by explaining that this faith in the credible reproduction, the copy that conveys essence, was complemented by increasing anxiety over the remoteness of "authentic" experience, the sensation that modern America was rapidly becoming, in E. L. Godkin's memorable phrase, a "chromocivilization."[28] These twin impulses—one that identifies with the technological culture of reliable facsimiles, another that expresses nostalgia over the loss of authenticity—permeate the literary record of American realism, causing writers such as Mark Twain to appear like

reluctant phrenologists. Twain firmly believed that emerging technologies of print and image reproduction, such as the Paige Typesetter
and the Kalaotype process, would revolutionize human communication, even to the point that words would someday become unnecessary obstacles to the transmission of information.[29] Yet this abiding
faith in the power of technology to devise increasingly transparent
forms of representation aroused his sense of nostalgia for a world of
childhood experience, full of original sensation. It is not a coincidence
that the phrenologists and fortune-tellers that appear so often in his
fiction are, with few exceptions, either malicious con men or bum-
bling frauds.[30] Twain's confidence in the culture of reproduction is
matched by profound skepticism about the reliability of any act of
mimetic performance.

   Caricature, the period's other great representational preoccupa-
tion, entertained these dual commitments to reproduction and
authenticity with equal ambivalence through the motif of the "Phrenologist Coon" (figure I.4). Of course, the art of caricature has traditionally maintained strong ties to the academic study of physiog-

FIGURE I.4. "The
Phrenologist Coon,"
Department of Special
Collections, Knight Library,
University of Oregon.

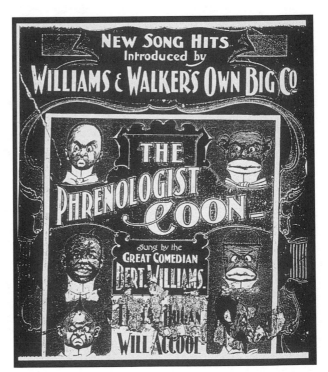

nomy, the science of reading facial features as indices of character and temperament. Seventeenth- and eighteenth-century researchers such as Johan Lavater and Charles le Brun devised elaborate genealogies linking the human types to their animal and vegetable origins, a project that generated some of the Enlightenment's most intriguing caricatures and that provided models for the more self-consciously humorous images of the nineteenth century.[31] Like realism, caricature operates on the phrenological and physiognomic premise that the essence of identity can be gleaned through observation and interpretation of the exterior form. The "Phrenologist Coon" of Ernest Hogan's popular song applies this clinical logic in a compelling analysis of his own ethnic identity.

> Of all the men in history,
> 'Tis said I'se the mystery!
> As conjureman I'se the king!
> For I'se well versed in psychology,
> Knows all about phrenology,
> In ethnology I'se the thing. . . .
> Now by us scientists 'tis often said,
> If a coon has an egg-shaped head
> Means chicken he will steal! . . .
> If his head's shaped like a razor,
> You can bet that coon will cut;
> If his head looks like a billy goat,
> Beware, dat coon will butt. [32]

This intriguing example of "coon"-era songcraft betrays ethnic caricature's ambivalence about the legibility of human essences and underscores one of the form's crucial affinities with realism. Hogan's lyrics insist that the phrenologist, like the caricaturist who renders his image on the sheet music score, successfully deciphers the physiognomic markers that signify "coon" identity. The singer's additional credentials in the sciences of conjure, psychology, and ethnology bestow an aura of professional legitimacy on his efforts to trace cranial features to their ethnic sources. Yet the song evokes this dehumanizing logic only to mock its leading assumptions, for instead of phrenological interpretation, the singer actually engages in something more like free association with ethnic clichés. Egg connotes a love of chicken; razor connotes a willingness to cut. The second term in these simple equations brings "the essential man" no closer to view than the first, for both the shape of the head and the character it purportedly expresses are interchangeable conventions for an already thoroughly conventional notion of "coon" identity. The song, in other words, betrays phrenology as a form of quackery—perhaps, in Hogan's view, a close disciplinary cousin of ethnology, psychology, and conjure— even as it applies the unambiguously racist logic of phrenological practice. Like American realism, ethnic caricature dwells in this ambivalence over the nature of originality and replication, at times insisting on a rigid teleology of race, at other times emphasizing the fluid, symbolic quality of ostensible racial identifiers. The "phrenologist coon," like the reluctant phrenologist of literary realism, is a figure for this ambivalence, an assertion of racial hierarchy and, at the same time, a demonstration of racial indeterminacy. It should come as no surprise that both Hogan and the song's best known performer, Bert Williams, were erudite black men, whose conflicted relation to the conventions of "coon" comedy was at least as problematic as Mark Twain's investment in the culture of reproduction.

The late nineteenth-century illustrated periodical provided a site for such ambivalent gestures by both the literary realist and the ethnic caricaturist. Among the literary periodicals, *Harper's Monthly* had been the first to recognize the potential of illustration to transform the size and function of the magazine industry. Employing artists and engravers at terrific expense, the magazine wedded literature to illustration in the 1850s, reaching out to a broad audience with a product calculated to appeal to even marginally cultivated readers. Other major literary periodicals, such as *Scribner's Monthly* and later *Century,* caught on to the vogue for graphic entertainment, and dozens of new illustrated weeklies emerged to satisfy the public appetite for journalistic art.[33] A few of the older periodicals, including the *Atlantic Monthly* and the *North American Review,* held out against the rest, but such conservatism was rare. Fulkerson, the fictional publisher of an upstart literary magazine in Howells's *A Hazard of New Fortunes,* hints at the pervasiveness of the trend when he exclaims that only a "lunatic" would open a magazine "in the twilight of the nineteenth century *without* illustrations."[34] A literary traditionalist in many respects himself, Howells had left the starchy *Atlantic* a few years before *Hazard*'s publication in 1890 to assume an editorial job with the lavishly illustrated *Harper's.* Even Henry James, who professed deep misgivings about the role of visual images in relation to the literary text, was compelled to observe that "[t]he illustration of books, and even more of magazines, may be said to have been born in our time, so far as variety and abundance are the signs of it; or born, at any rate, the comprehensive, ingenious, sympathetic spirit in which we conceive and practice it."[35]

Improvements in the technology of print reproduction during the second half of the nineteenth century had made the *Harper's* revolution possible. The introduction of wood engraving as a substitute for the cumbersome and expensive process of inscribing steel plates had dramatically reduced overhead costs, enabling even fledgling publishing ventures to produce limited numbers of affordable images. For all its economy, the new process still involved the coordinated efforts of an artist, who produced the original image or, more often, a faithful copy of some classic painting, and a skilled engraver, who transferred the image to a wooden block. Quality work of this sort required very deep pockets, as dozens of short-lived illustrated magazines discovered. *Century*, which produced first-rate wood engravings throughout the 1880s and 1890s, spent approximately $5,000 per month on its art department, a figure that would have been inconceivable to the magazine's smaller competitors. For most of a generation, as images of various kinds and of mixed quality proliferated in American magazines, *Harper's, Century, Scribner's* and a few other well-established periodicals set the standard for print illustration.[36]

The introduction of photoengraving during the late 1880s and early 1890s sparked a second wave of revolution and brought an end to the reign of the "quality" literary periodicals over the sphere of magazine art. By using photographic images to create reproducible plates, the "half-tone" process made both the artist and the engraver obsolete, paving the way for a new generation of garishly illustrated, remarkably inexpensive, and terrifically popular magazines. During the summer of 1893, the premier issue of *McClure's* arrived on newsstands with a price tag of fifteen cents, *Cosmopolitan* sold for twelve, and two-year-old *Munsey's Magazine* dropped its price to ten cents per issue.[37] "The revolution in the art of engraving, not to say its destruction," announced one commentator in 1895, "is threatening a change in the conduct of monthly magazines." This cautious assessment understated the crisis facing the more expensive literary periodicals (*Harper's* sold for thirty-five cents in 1893), which could no longer take for granted the superior number and quality of their graphic offerings. Gilder theorized that the novelty of photoengraving would eventually wear out, and he predicted that readers would return to the magazines that featured original images, executed by artists and engravers. Nevertheless, by 1893 one-third of the images in Gilder's own *Century Magazine,* half of those in *Harper's,* and as many as two-thirds of those in *Scribner's* were produced through photoengraving. Two years later, an editor at *McClure's,* which published only halftone images, took evident pride in observing that "less than one-seventh of the illustrations in last month's *Harper's, Century,* and *Scribner's* are engraved on wood."[38]

Caricature flourished in this unique climate of transition, as the older periodicals scrambled to modernize in the face of unprecedented competition and a rapidly changing marketplace.[39] Traditionally viewed as the crudest of arts, graphic caricature had played almost no part in the rise of the major literary periodicals, which had devoted their artistic resources to more elevated themes, such as travel, portraiture, military conquest, and European art. As the influence of the "quality" periodicals reached its highest point during the 1870s, a lively discourse of American caricature had begun to take root in the more plebeian weeklies, but the coarse humor of magazines such as *Harper's Weekly* showed no signs of penetrating the genteel sphere presided over by the company's more austere monthly periodical.

Nevertheless, by the late 1880s, pressured by technological and economic forces beyond their control, art departments at some of the older magazines began to regard caricature in a new light. Simple line drawings and cartoon etchings were a form of "original" art— a throwback to the glory days of engraving—that was both popular with readers and cheap to reproduce. John Ames Mitchell proved just how cheap in 1883 by establishing the enormous success of *Life* magazine on the strength of another technological innovation, the zinc etching process, which allowed artists to reproduce black and white line drawings directly, instead of having them engraved on wooden blocks.[40] Moreover, as Thomas Nast's images of Tammany Hall corruption in New York had begun to demonstrate during the 1870s, the bold lines of a well-conceived caricature were an extraordinarily articulate editorial tool. Unwilling to yield entirely to the new order of photographic reproduction, yet aware that the elaborate original engravings of the 1860s and 1870s were no longer economically viable, art departments at the older literary periodicals joined innovators such as Mitchell in embracing the art of caricature as both a concession to, and an expression of, contemporary conditions.

This concession was not offered all at once, and editors were at first content to incorporate caricature less as a graphic technique than as a topic of analysis. Throughout the late 1880s and early 1890s, *Century* entertained readers with caricatured images disguised in the form of scholarship, publishing illustrated essays on subjects such as "Early Political Caricature in America," "In Bohemia with George Du Maurier," and "A German Comic Paper: *Fliegende Blätter.*" Never willing to be outdone, *Harper's* followed suit with a lavish facsimile of the "Unpublished Letters of Thackeray," complete with the author's humorous sketches. Other periodicals quickly mimicked the trick, and by 1891 even the stoic *Review of Reviews* had learned to finesse its print-only editorial policy by introducing an annual graphic feature entitled "A Year's History in Caricature," which soon became "The Month in Caricature" in response to popular demand. A subject that had received virtually no scholarly attention in the United States before 1880 suddenly compelled wide interest among commentators, who flooded the literary journals with essays on such topics as "The Growth of Caricature" (*The Critic,* 1882), "Caricature, the Fantastic, the Grotesque"(*Littell's Living Age,* 1888), "Popular Caricature" (*The Saturday Review,* 1888), "Contemporary American Caricature" (*Scribner's,* 1889), "Our Caricaturists and Cartoonists" (*Munsey's,* 1894), "Technical Tendencies of Caricature" (*The Quarterly Illustrator,* 1895), "Moral Reflections on Burlesque Art" (*The Quarterly Illustrator,* 1895), and "What Is Caricature?" (*Littell's Living Age,* 1899).[41] James followed suit, perhaps reluctantly, by composing a retrospective essay titled "Daumier, Caricaturist" for *Century* in 1890.[42]

Amid this explosion of interest, ethnic caricatures made up only a small percentage of the total repertoire of comic images that began to appear with increasing frequency in the quality periodicals. The "Editor's Drawer" column in *Harper's,* tucked at the end of each number, became a popular repository for dialect humor and comic images of ethnic figures, such as the laughable newlyweds of Peter Newell's 1893 illustration "A Valuable Suggestion" (figure I.5).[43] Genteel anti-Semitism tended to be a more discreet affair, but the stereotypical bearded and unkempt Jew made an occasional appearance, and *Century* poked fun at the shortcomings of the Irish in regular illustrated features, such as the barely legible "Drusil's Fairf'" (figure I.6). Far more common than such deliberately exaggerated images were documentary illustrations of the various ethnic "types," illustrations that spoke with even greater authority than their humorous counterparts because of their evident seriousness. Images of this variety were never overtly dehumanizing, but if caricature is less a formal quality of certain representations than a process of defining the individual in terms of its relation to an abstract principle, then images such as J. Campbell Phillips's "A Pickaninny" can properly be understood as an important element in the growth of caricature as a form of genteel entertainment (figure I.7). At least one commentator of the period was willing to make this conceptual leap, defining caricature broadly as "the forcing of characteristics to emphasize expression."[44] Whether this "forcing" involved comic exaggeration or more subtle forms of graphic coercion, much of the magazine art published by the better periodicals after 1890 depicted ethnic, cultural, or class "characteristics" as determining features of identity, suggesting that individuals are traceable to certain generic sources, and that "type" is the hidden truth behind the illusion of "character."

FIGURE I.5. Peter Newell, "A Valuable Suggestion," *Harper's Monthly* 87 (November 1893): 971.

A VALUABLE SUGGESTION.
By-Stander (*to the bridegroom*). "Say, Lem, yer orter wear 'spendahs on you' gloves to hol' 'em up."

Drawn by J. Campbell Phillips
A PICKANINNY

FIGURE 1.6. J. Campbell Phillips,
"A Pickaninny,"
The Quarterly Illustrator
4 (May 1895).

At the same time that advances in image technology were establishing new standards for graphic content in the traditional monthlies, standards to which caricature was uniquely adapted, literary realism asserted a parallel claim on the critical sensibilities of editors at *Harper's, Century,* and *Scribner's.* Moreover, as with the growth of caricature, realism took root in the older monthlies as both an expression of and a form of resistance to the emerging mass culture of the 1890s. Richard Ohmann has effectively described the profound "cultural divide" separating the demure look and tone of *Harper's*

FIGURE 1.7. "Drusil,"
Century 48 (July 1894): 506.

Monthly in 1880 from the snappy, immediate experience offered by *Munsey's Magazine* just fifteen years later.[45] Whereas *Munsey's* introduced middle-class readers to a world of commodities and leisure activities that promised to constitute a better life, *Harper's* addressed an audience that possessed culture already and wished to see it carefully preserved. Having pioneered the complementary practices of photoengraving and yellow journalism, the irrepressible Frank Munsey declared that the older periodicals appeared "made for anaemics," and he accused editors such as Henry Mills Alden of *Harper's* and Thomas Bailey Aldrich of the *Atlantic Monthly* of "living in an artificial literary world . . . which woefully lacked human interest."[46]

Walter Hines Page, an *Atlantic* editor who went on to found one of the new magazines, *The World's Work,* coined the phrase "homely realism" to describe the emerging editorial spirit, which called for "more directness, more clearness" than was fashionable in the "leisurely style of a generation or two ago."[47] Topical rather than conversational, informative rather than diverting, sassy rather than cheerful, the new magazines made an overt appeal to educated, recently affluent, middle-class readers by wooing this underdeveloped consumer group with fast-paced articles and exposes on technology, politics, industry, and entertainment. The "literary" component of newcomers like *McClure's* was similarly designed to grab, rather than cultivate, the attention of readers, who, in the magazine's opinion, were no longer interested in "washed out studies of effete human nature."[48] Advertising copy, previously regarded as a minor embarrassment, occupied as much as 25 percent of printed space in the modern magazines and became increasingly indistinguishable from content. Advertisers and editors alike treated written words as commercial instruments and valued them, according to Christopher Wilson, "in direct proportion to their clarity, 'strength,' and above all, their ability to persuade."[49]

Against such competition, the old literary periodicals had little choice but to change, and Howellsian realism offered a compelling, if problematic, blend of the new and old orders. In aligning their editorial practices with the "modern" aesthetic of realism, magazines such as *Harper's* and *Scribner's* could represent themselves as advance units in a democratic revolt against the genteel literary culture that had unapologetically ignored "real" experience in favor of enduring values. Howells enlisted recruits for his "realism war" by casting the spirit of European romanticism as the natural adversary of "democracy in literature," but his campaign for realism was really part of an internal struggle to transform the fading old monthlies into viable media enterprises.[50] Under the combined banner of realism and democracy, the quality magazines proposed to widen the lens of American consciousness, opening to view the real lives of real citizens in their everyday pursuits. "Art," Howells wrote from the "Editor's Study" at *Harper's,* "is beginning to find out that if it does not make friends with Need it must perish."[51]

Howells understood that "Art," though not always recognizable as such, adapts almost instantly to new social and economic realities, as the richly illustrated advertisements in *Munsey's Magazine* had already proven to anyone who cared to notice. Howells really meant that *Harper's* and other institutions like it would "perish" if they did not change, and he was right. Largely through his efforts, the older periodicals did change by incorporating into their aesthetic design the experience of middle- and lower-class characters, the regional idiosyncrasies of rural figures, the plight of urban immigrants, "the mass of common men," wherever they might live in "simplicity, naturalness, and honesty."[52] In embracing "the worth of the vulgar," Howells, Gilder, and other progressive editors had no intention of dissolving the social order, any more than they wished to see moral and aesthetic standards handed over to Frank Munsey's masspublic.[53] As Amy Kaplan has so persuasively shown, realism operated for these editors as a means to challenge both the genteel tradition of exclusion based on class and ethnic difference *and* the even more pressing threat of intrusion by a modern consumer ethos that measured aesthetic value in dollars alone.[54] With its highly selective openness to social reality, realism of the sort endorsed by the periodicals defined itself against both the conservatism of *The North American Review* and the muckraking excesses of *Munsey's* and *McClure's,* carving out a thin but significant niche in the dynamic cultural situation of the 1890s. Much as graphic caricature reconciled new technologies with old aesthetic values, magazine realism of the same period served the interests of democracy and of patriarchy at once, instituting new controls over the representation of formerly invisible subjects in the act of making them visible.

Gilder's refusal to print the word "dynamite" in the pages of *Century* for fear of inciting anarchy, like his famous bowdlerization of an installment from *Huckleberry Finn,* hints at the managerial spirit with which the quality magazines confidently represented something they called "reality." But realism's democratization of American literary taste introduced more systemic controls, as well, and here it is possible to observe an immediate form of interaction between the aesthetic projects of realism and caricature. Indeed, the art of caricature may have been the era's bluntest and most effective means of policing itself in the domain of class and ethnic representation, for caricature's humorous excesses allowed magazines such as *Century* to address the demand for "real life" while ensuring that undesirable elements of "reality" remained at a safe distance. The magazine frequently published stories of life among the ghettos of the North and the white-washed cabins of the South, extending realism's sympathetic reach to ethnic types ignored in the elitist fiction of the previous generation. For all its sympathy, however, *Century* followed the example of *Harper's* and *Scribner's* in routinely drawing upon a vocabulary of brutal ethnic clichés to complete the finer point of its representation of the "vulgar" elements in American society (figures I.8 and I.9). As a technique of realist literary performance, both within and in relation to the literary text, caricature served to insulate readers from the potentially unnerving social "reality" that the magazine made a point of opening to view. In a moment of intriguing candor, *Century*'s publisher, Roswell Smith, expressed hope that the realistic emphasis in contemporary fiction would marginalize revolutionary elements in the social fabric, helping to "postpone if not prevent the great impending struggle between labor and capital."[55] As a strategic corrective to the magazine's democratizing impulse, and as a basic feature of realist literary practice, ethnic caricature played an important role in Smith's postponement scheme.

The exaggerated ethnic abstractions that proliferated in the older magazines after 1890 already had a solid footing in American culture by the time Gilder and Howells began to incorporate them into the design of the literary monthlies. In fact, magazines such as *Harper's* introduced few modifications to a lexicon of graphic conventions that was widely in use among the vibrant weekly papers by the early 1880s. Some of those conventions were inherited directly from British, French, and German sources—the simian traits of the poor Irish-American, for example, are evident in much older British caricatures—whereas others took shape in the pages of *Harper's Weekly, Truth, Life,* and similar papers.[56] Foremost in contributing to this burgeoning discourse of ethnic caricature were a new breed of humor magazines that grew up in response to the public's seemingly unlimited appetite for graphic comedy. *Puck,* which began publishing in 1877, led all others with the quality of its illustrations and the

FIGURE 1.8. E. W. Kemble, "Charlie and the Possum,"
Century 46 (May 1892): 159.

FIGURE 1.9. "Twas Ever Thus," *Scribner's Monthly* 13 (April 1877): 432.

intelligence of its political and social satire, whereas *Judge,* founded in 1881 by a group of *Puck* artists and editors, was a worthy rival.[57] Caricature constituted the principal mode of editorial discourse in these magazines, which employed the latest techniques in chromolithography to produce some of the era's most remarkable and unsettling journalistic art. Although they sparred good-naturedly over local and national politics, both magazines boasted an unflappable conservatism on basic social and economic issues. Despite the solid Republicanism of *Judge* and the pro-Cleveland sympathies of *Puck,* there existed throughout the period an underlying consensus on the value of honest work, patriotism, common sense, and masculine authority, a consensus often articulated through graphic attacks on groups perceived to be lacking in such essential components of American citizenship.[58]

Even prior to the emergence of *Puck, Judge,* and *Life,* the era's third great comic paper, American political caricature had involved a significant ethnic dimension. A representative lithograph from 1844 depicts Uncle Sam as Ben Franklin, outraged to discover that the child of Liberty is being nursed by abolitionists, blacks, and traitors (figure I.10). In campaign images from the 1860 presidential election, Republicans and Democrats traded ethnic insults, each party accusing the other of offering African Americans a scandalously prominent role in the party platform. Such illustrations anticipated the social and aesthetic logic of late nineteenth-century ethnic caricature by defining American political identity against an exaggerated representation of racial difference, none more effectively than an 1860 Democratic campaign image entitled "An Heir to the Throne, or the Next Republican Candidate" (figure I. 11). On display as one of P. T. Barnum's famous oddities, the diminutive black figure emphasizes the perfect incompatibility of the "higher" and "lower" races by turning Barnum's slogan "What is it?" against his Republican supporters with the slang rejoinder "What can dey be?"

Throughout the Reconstruction era, graphic commentators of every political stripe repeated some version of this joke, employing images of ethnic difference to contest the boundaries of American citizenship. Even Nast's pioneering images of injustice at Tammany Hall were unquestionably fueled by his rabid hatred of the Irish, which boiled over in illustrations that depict an Irish-Catholic menace to the very foundations of American liberty.[59] Nast's famous illustration "The Ignorant Vote" posited a graphic balance between twin forms of savagery in the national electorate, offering the possibility

FIGURE I.10. "A Boston Notion for the World's Fair—A New Cradle of Liberty," reprinted without attribution in Joseph B. Bishop, "Early Political Caricature in America," *Century* 44 (1891): 219–31.

that America's Northern and Southern proletarian classes might effectively cancel one another's political participation (figure I.12).

Such aggressive condescension intended to bolster confidence in the dominant culture's ability to perpetuate the status quo. Historians of the Gilded Age, such as T. Jackson Lears and Tom Lutz, have described the fragility of this sense of confidence, suggesting that white middle-class anxieties were running unusually high at the close of the nineteenth century.[60] As affluent Americans flocked to sanatoriums and medical resorts to express their sense of dispossession in nervous suffering, middle-class urban whites turned to the more affordable pages of *Harper's Weekly* or *Puck* for a different sort of medicine, one designed to codify social distinctions in an atmosphere of debilitating uncertainty. An 1891 illustration in *Life* conveyed the editorial spirit of the age by depicting an elfin monarch seated on a monumental throne, flanked by Art and Literature, who prepare to depict the racial and ethnic types assembled at the foot of

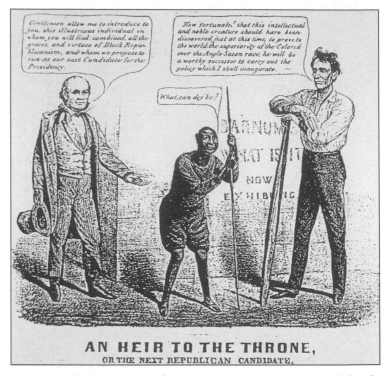

FIGURE I.II. "An Heir to the Throne, or the Next Republican Candidate," reprinted without attribution in Bishop, "Early Political Caricature in America," *Century* 44 (1891): 219–31.

the stairs (figure I.13). Ethnic caricature, the image implies, functions as a strategic control on the magazine's own democratic experiment, ensuring that ethnic identities remain fixed and discernible in the bewildering flux of a multiethnic society. The impressive power of exaggerated ethnic images to check the advance of alienism against a childlike, romanticized image of the bourgeois self is enacted and, in a sense, betrayed in this utterly self-conscious caricature of the functions of ethnic caricature.

The *Life* image treats ethnic identity as a vaguely threatening potential, easily mastered by the magazine's editorial policies, but in practice ethnic caricature involved subtle distinctions between the kinds and magnitudes of alienism represented by the various human "types." African Americans, for example, were generally represented in the journalistic art of the period as eager but unqualified candidates for assimilation to white middle-class norms, their efforts at

FIGURE I.12. Thomas Nast, "The Ignorant Vote—Honors Are Easy,"
Harper's Weekly (December 9, 1876).

racial mimicry or masquerade only confirming the traditional em-
beddedness of black Americans within a system of material commodities. *Puck*'s 1880 image "Wool-Gathering," which conflates the
black Southern laborer with the product of his labor, constitutes an
early example of the trope E. W. Kemble would later institutionalize
as the very essence of "coon" caricature (figure I.14).[61]

Kemble played this graphic joke for all it was worth by staging
the endless tribulations of uppity black figures who cannot escape a
family resemblance with the livestock they tend. His "A is fo Amos"
in *A Coon Alphabet* carefully triangulates the mule's elongated ears
with the rabbit-like headpiece of the mother and the angled brim of
the boy's hat to create a ludicrous menagerie (figures I.15 and I.16).
The mother's evident pride and the dandyish attitude of the boy are
effectively chastened when his trip to school produces not social mobility but a violent repetition of the dehumanizing analogy of the

FIGURE 1.13. "*Life* Receives the New Year," *Life* 17 (January 1, 1891), 10.

opening image. The boy's flailing legs as he disappears into the school door are a visual reminder of his inescapable kinship with the kicking mule, whose scholarly demeanor suggests at least an equal capacity for successful assimilation.

If such imagery makes the black subject inseparable from its material context, confusing men and mules in a calculated rejection of the subject's humanity, Jews were also portrayed as insufficiently human, though for different reasons.[62] Whereas African Americans typically appear as ineffectual masqueraders, bad actors who are fundamentally interchangeable with the material commodities they so

FIGURE 1.14. "Wool-Gathering," *Puck* (April 28, 1880), 128.

FIGURES 1.15–16. E. W. Kemble, "A is fo Amos," *A Coon Alphabet*
New York: R. H. Russell, 1899).

closely resemble, the Jew in late nineteenth-century American caricature forfeits his claim to humanity by expressing an unlimited
willingness to commodify everyone and everything around him.
When Levi learns of his son's death on the railroad in a typical *Judge*
cartoon from 1892, he can muster emotion only for the money he
will collect in damages. A Jewish tailor in *Puck*'s "Profitable Benevolence" offers to clothe a destitute fellow citizen, but this apparent act
of human kindness only completes the victim's reification, trans-
forming the unwitting sufferer into a walking advertisement for
Cohn's tailor shop (figure I.17).

Images of the African American who is incapable of emerging
fully from a material state and of the Jew who perpetrates such dehumanizing tricks on others frame a zone of "authentic" selfhood
that late nineteenth-century magazine readers claimed as their own.
Whether such images appeared as full-page humorous assaults in
the weekly comic papers or as modest filler items in the more somber pages of *Harper's Monthly,* illustrations of the irreparably subhuman African American and of the excessively acquisitive Jew—
dehumanized and dehumanizing extremes in an imaginary cultural
spectrum—marked the outer edges of an inherently privileged bourgeois identity, reserving the ideal of an autonomous, sympathetic, and
creative self as the racial prerogative of white middle-class Americans.
Life invited readers to dwell in this imaginatively privileged cultural
center by depicting a lavishly adorned black woman, whose companion worries that such an excessive display of jewelry will disguise her

FIGURE I.17. "Profitable Benevolence," *Puck* (March 20, 1901).

PROFITABLE BENEVOLENCE

" Here, my poor man. I ain'd godt der heart to see anypody go
coldt : pud dis on und vear it!

" Ach ! Who says der Heprew haf no heart? "

"nationality" (figure I.18). "How so, Mister Jackson?" she inquires, to which he responds, "You'll be took fo' a Jewess." This two-pronged punch line emphasizes the impossibility of mistaking "Miss Saffron" for anything but a "coon," a graphic conclusion that stigmatizes the materialism of the Jew as much as it does the materiality of the African American. Other ethnic subjects lent unique forms of support to this calculus of racial identity by exhibiting their unfitness for assimilation in exaggerated contortions. The Russian or German anarchist who prefers dynamite to democracy, the Indian who can dress like an American but cannot relinquish his appetite for raw meat, the Irishman who spends his generous government pension on whiskey: each of these figures, and many more, served to delineate the boundaries of legitimate citizenship for a culture unsure of its claim to authority. By denying sentient personhood to others, the caricaturist shored up the embattled bourgeois self, restoring confidence in the unstable margins of a vaguely discernible "American" identity.

Yet if the period's rich discourse of ethnic misrepresentation provided defensive cover for the self-authorizing fantasies of "white" Americans, the very form of these misrepresentations introduced contradictory meanings as well. Indeed, the ironies circulating through Ernest Hogan's "Phrenologist Coon" convey an impression

FIGURE 1.18. E. W. Kemble's illustration appeared originally in *Life* and was reprinted in *Coontown's 400* (New York: Life Publishing, 1899).

of the rival impulses inherent to the caricatured image, as Robert Fletcher has explained. Describing Thackeray's illustrations for *Henry Esmond,* he maintains that "the caricaturist's art brings separate impressions (norm and deviation) into juxtaposition, and thus highlights the constructedness of perceptual reality."[63] Gombrich and Ernst Kris agree that the caricatured image paradoxically articulates social and behavioral norms, even as "the abbreviated style gains its own significance" by casting suspicion on the integrity of the representation.[64] An effective caricature may signify the inferiority of some individual or group by elaborating on "deviations" from the social norm, but the insubstantiality of the caricatured image, its exaggerated artificiality, is itself a rebuke to the very idea of the norm. Caricature's "abbreviated style," as Gombrich and Kris observe, poses an internal challenge to the integrity of social or conceptual hierarchies that the caricatured image may be designed to support.

This inherent paradox is even more acutely pronounced in the context of the ethnic image, which served late nineteenth-century readers so efficiently as a pillar of bourgeois self-understanding, despite the subversive potential of a self-consciously "constructed" visual field. That subversive potential is on display in Eugene Zimmerman's compelling self-portrait, "The Vampires of Thought," which depicts the violence of exaggerated ethnic representation through an analogy with the vampire's consumption of human blood (figure I.19). Waking in the middle of the night, not with thirst but with a bright idea, the artist metaphorically sustains himself by drawing the life out of others, in this case the hapless Irishman with his ubiquitous goat. But if the illustration abstractly evokes the cannibalistic dimension of ethnic caricature, it is the vampire in this sketch who is rendered graphically according to the violent impulse of comic typification. His emaciated features and discarded collar hint at the artist's victimization, as if the logic of ethnic misrepresentation has exerted a reflexive influence over the caricaturist's self-portrait. Caricature here performs the dual function of empowering and disabling the artist's authority, a paradox "Zim" and others deployed for comic effect in countless illustrations that feature the caricaturist, no less than his ethnic subject, as a sort of monster.

Even when the artist/ethnologist remains out of view, ethnic images possess a reflexive capacity to dismantle elements of the perceptual field in the act of its construction. An 1884 installment in *Puck*'s "Streets of New York" series, for example, dramatizes the ten-

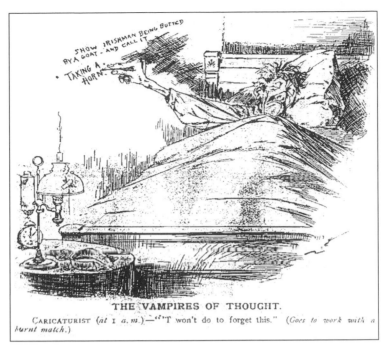

FIGURE I.19. Eugene Zimmerman, "The Vampires of Thought,"
Judge 17 (November 1889).

dency of reified ethnic images to become slippery as a consequence
of the caricaturist's success at reducing identity to a handful of racial
cues (figure I.20). The illustration depicts the representatives of three
purportedly savage races, an Indian, an Irishman, and an African
American, dressed as human advertisements in costumes that trans-
late racial identity into a series of clichés. The caption articulates the
sentiments of an industrious street worker, who gazes at the three
loafers and asks: "Why need we go to the Far West to enjoy the picturesqueness of the frontier when we see it every day in our own
city?" This sarcastic remark claims "our city" for white workers and
Puck readers, who wish it *were* necessary to travel to the Far West to
enjoy such degraded picturesqueness. Ridiculous ethnic costumes
accentuate the illustration's ample facial evidence that all three savages are unfit for existence on this side of the frontier. But, of course,
the mock-picturesqueness of the scene is a function of dramatic
representation, for instead of a "real" Indian, Irishman, or African
American, the illustration depicts self-conscious ethnic perform-

FIGURE 1.20. "The Streets of New York," *Puck* (December 3, 1884), 211.

ances by three paid actors, impersonators who perform menial roles in a marketing scheme. Standard props, swollen features, and silly costumes serve to exaggerate ethnic particularity, allowing readers to appreciate an unambiguous distinction between "us" and "them," but in its zeal to concretize that distinction the illustration blurs the lines of ethnic difference, for there is no guarantee that symbolic attire corresponds to ethnic reality. The real culprit in *Puck*'s clumsy satire is a consumer ethos that knows no boundaries, and that threatens to make individuals of every class and ethnicity into mere advertisements for an increasingly abstract conception of self.

The same paradox animates the asymmetrical game of chance featured on the frontispiece of this book. A nattily dressed gambler, a figure for the caricaturist who is also engaged in "playing the races," controls the deck. His intended victims regard him suspiciously, but they appear helpless to affect the outcome, which is scripted as much in their exaggerated facial features as in the cards that are surely stacked against them. Ethnic caricature, the image implies, is a losing game for the subject whose origin and destiny can be quickly sketched in thick lines and blotches of ink. But if the illustration makes an overt appeal to racist sensibilities by branding its ethnic subjects with conventional identifiers, it just as overtly represents ethnic identity as an insidious cultural fiction, perpetrated through manipulation and intimidation. Like Hogan's "Phrenologist Coon," the *Life* illustration deploys conventions of ethnic caricature to explode the myth of racial hierarchy, setting in motion the contradictory impulses that fuel the era's profound fascination with this sort of comedy. It is impossible to know if *Life's* readers responded more enthusiastically to the sketch's racist symbolism or to the undoing of that symbolism in the ludic extravagance of the caricatured image. In either case, the illustration serves to expose the nature of the game, even as it makes victims of the game's ethnic participants, generating in this complex process a form of ambivalence that can be read as the signature of late nineteenth-century ruminations on race and identity.

Harper's Monthly made no effort to compete with the comic weeklies for supremacy in the domain of ethnic caricature, and yet *Harper's* and other established literary monthlies actively participated in the era's discourse of comic typification by providing a forum in which leading writers and illustrators could explore and develop important affinities. It would be capricious to suggest that Howells, Mark Twain, Edith Wharton, or the other writers considered in this book derived techniques of literary representation directly from the exaggerated graphic images that often appeared alongside their fiction in the major monthlies. Nevertheless, each of these writers employed comic typification as a regular feature of realist practice, and their engagement with the art of ethnic caricature produced some of the period's most distinctive and problematic fiction. Mark Twain's representation of Jim in *Adventures of Huckleberry Finn* is the most celebrated and controversial instance of this curious overlap, but Howells's "Celtic army" in *Suburban Sketches,* James's "swarming" Hebrews and Italians in *The American Scene,* the "impossible" Jew of Wharton's *The House of Mirth,* the Irish brutes of Stephen Crane and Frank Norris, and Charles Chesnutt's obsequious Uncle Julius all betray literary realism's uncertain relation to the magazine culture that made ethnic caricature a staple element in late nineteenth-century American intellectual life.

The nature of such lapses in what Joel Chandler Harris called realism's "true function"—the faithful representation of "character" and "individuality"—has never been fully understood. Critics have often contended that Howells and his contemporaries were simply too squeamish or too blind to the proliferation of class tensions to approach them more directly, as if the caricatured image amounted to a botched attempt at mimesis by an author unfamiliar with his or her subject.[65] June Howard has challenged this characterization of realism's "inaccuracies," arguing that the writer's distortions of lower-class life deliberately reinscribe social hierarchies in the realm of literary representation.[66] Kaplan further explains that the shadowy aliens in fiction by Howells, Dreiser, and Wharton serve to dispel a powerful sensation of "unreality" festering at the heart of middle-class life.[67] Like the graphic caricaturist, the literary realist populates the frontiers of a precariously constructed "real" world with the distorted bodies and faces of patently unreal ethnic "types," who neatly define the colorful fringes of social reality. No less than *Puck,* the realist novel, according to this analysis, is inversely constituted by the boldly sketched ethnic "types" that exist just beyond the pale of realist representation.

This argument goes a long way toward explaining the functions of ethnic caricature within the context of American literary realism, but it tells only part of the story. Exaggerated ethnic images, such as "The Phrenologist Coon," possess an uncanny reflexive quality, one that serves to contest the same bourgeois mythology that such images were ostensibly devised to empower. There is no question that Hogan's "coon" characterization deploys a racist convention, and yet the song treats phrenology itself—the idea that essences are outwardly legible—as a cultural fiction. Do we understand the "coon" of Hogan's song as evidence of a culturally discernible foundation from which the "individual" develops outward, and to which it might be reliably traced, or is the "coon" always a mere performance, a fictional overlay for the multiple attitudes of a fluid and essentially unknowable identity? The major figures of American literary realism were drawn to ethnic caricature because the mode sets in motion such basic questions about the nature of self and identity in the context of late nineteenth-century consumer culture. Caricature surely performed a defensive function, stabilizing the realist's social vision against threats of upheaval from outside, but James, Twain, Dreiser, Wharton, Chesnutt, and Crane were at least as intrigued by the power of caricature to disturb an excessively complacent social vision by entertaining the possibility that identity may be entirely a performative affair.

Given that the art of ethnic misrepresentation served such uncertain commitments, it is not surprising that the exaggerated ethnic image in realist fiction typically raises more questions than it answers. When Howells in *An Imperative Duty,* for example, describes a group of black "dandies" whose outlandish attire gives them "that air of being clothed through and through, as to the immortal spirit as well as the perishable body," he is fully in step with popular "coon" representations of the period.[68] These perplexing figures are rigidly delineated as ethnic "types," for only a "coon," the passage implies, would take such pride in the ridiculous display of loud colors and shiny fabrics. Yet although their exaggerated attention to appearance serves as an index to "coon" identity, fixing these social misfits in their proper place, the passage just as deliberately insists that such extravagant clothing operates as a precariously unstable signifier. To be "clothed through and through, as to the immortal spirit as well as the perishable body," is to lack an ethnic or class essence that might be expressed in outward appearance, for the same attributes that make these dandies easily recognizable also make them utterly inscrutable. Ethnic caricature appeals to Howells, despite his strong misgivings about the ethics and aesthetics of literary typology, because the exaggerated ethnic image affords his distraught protagonist a measure of social confidence, even as it articulates Howells's profound ambivalence about the stability of the self and the nature of inherited social prestige. For writers who shared Howells's complex sympathies, the image of black dandies who are continuous with their gaudy clothing offered a unique opportunity to critique the self-assurance of late nineteenth-century consumer culture, while enjoying whatever comfort there was to be taken from its guarantees of social privilege.

In the pages that follow, I will have a great deal more to say about the "complex sympathies" that underlie literary realism's investment in the art of ethnic caricature. In the meantime, I can perhaps clarify the major contours of my argument by suggesting an analogy with Werner Sollors's *Beyond Ethnicity,* a work of recent scholarship whose conceptual rigor I can only hope to emulate.[69] Raising a question that resonates with my own interest in the relationship between realism and caricature, Sollors asks how it is possible that "the concepts of the self-made man and of Jim Crow had their origins in the same culture at about the same time" (38). He notes that consent-based accounts of cultural identity, which assume that anyone can become an American or a member of the middle class simply by deciding to do so, "coexisted with countervailing rigidities" that emphasized conditions of natural descent (38). Sollors portrays late nineteenth-century America as a culture thoroughly enmeshed in contradiction over the rival claims of these two accounts of identity, and he details the ingenious maneuvers of intellectuals committed to forging an awkward synthesis. Josiah Royce's concept of "wholesome provincialism," which intended to steer a middle path between the twin evils of "ancient narrowness" and "the overwhelming forces of consolidation," was one such maneuver, designed to "save the individual" in a time of unique crisis (179). Randolph Bourne advanced a similar formula with the phrase "Trans-National America," which intended to reconcile the impulses of old nationalism and new cosmopolitanism within a unified structure of identity. Complaining that "our cities are filled with these half-breeds who retain their foreign names but have lost their foreign savor," Bourne proposed "trans-nationalism" as a form of hyphenate citizenship that would allow Americans to recover their ancestral ethnic and cultural specificity without reverting to the destructive tribal affiliations of the past (183). The goal for Royce, Bourne, and other intellectuals of the period was to carve out a conceptual role for inherited ethnic identity in a modern democratic society structured, in theory at least, by consensual relations. According to one commentator, the riddle of American identity could be solved only by navigating a course between "the Scylla of aggressive jingoism and the Charybdis of a denationalized cosmopolitanism" (191).

Late nineteenth-century ethnic caricature, whether it appears in *Puck* or in a novel by Henry James, constitutes another of the era's awkward, contradictory, and even duplicitous attempts to reconcile the rival claims of consent and descent in a coherent account of American identity.[70] With crude insistence, the caricatured image performs the cultural work of Bourne's "trans-nationalism," restoring to Bourne's savorless immigrants a keen and unavoidable awareness of their ethnic specificity. Against the unwelcome homogenization of the melting pot, caricature inscribes ethnic markers as inflexible features of identity, which only become more pronounced with every comical step the irreparable alien takes toward the fantasy of perfect assimilation. In affirming ethnic identity as a permanent birthright of the "mick," the "coon," the "kike," and the "wop," however, caricature reifies those categories so thoroughly that an alternative model of identity inevitably emerges as a dimension of the caricatured image, an improvisational, fluid cosmopolitanism that understands ethnicity as nothing more substantial than a comic performance. Ethnic caricature, like Bourne's internally conflicted notion of "trans-nationalism," accommodates these unlikely conceptual bedfellows in an economical image, allowing artists such as E. W. Kemble, no less than James himself, to represent identity as both given and made, handed down though the ages and constructed in the moment of its enactment.

In each of the ensuing chapters, I will be arguing that ethnic caricature appealed to the major figures of American literary realism both for its nativist impulse, which these writers shared, and for its potential to instigate a radical decentering of identity. In linking these parallel but antithetical gestures of the caricatured image, my argument echoes the position taken by another pathbreaking scholar of ethnicity, Michael North, who explains in *The Dialect of Modernism* that American writers of the early twentieth century often articulated their knottiest aesthetic concerns about the stability of language and representation through acts of ethnic mimicry, appropriation, and embodiment.[71] North's analysis has provided an indispensable model for my own, yet his impression that modernists such as Stein, Pound, and Eliot deployed jazz-inflected rhythms as a revolutionary affront to the conservatism of their Victorian forebears overlooks the special symbolic uses of alienism at the heart of Victorian literary culture in America. The "nigger drummer," "all teeth and lips," who chants enigmatically in Hemingway's *The Sun Also Rises,* Cather's Blind D'Arnault, the freakish musical prodigy who has "almost no head at all," the perfectly immobile "nigger on a mule," stationed like a ironic sentinel along the corridor to Faulkner's South, these ethnic grotesques are modern adaptations of a representational tradition that is at least as old as the antebellum minstrel show, a tradition whose mainstream literary expression originates in American realism's complex encounters with the art of ethnic caricature.[72]

In fact, North had legitimate reasons for ignoring the formal practice of ethnic caricature as a dimension of modernist literary experimentation, for by 1918 the caricatured image no longer commanded a wide American audience. *Puck* ceased to exist that year, as the photographic image sealed its authority over the popular imagination, and the elaborate, colorful caricatures of the 1890s came to seem as antiquated as the panoramic woodcuts of the previous generation. Nevertheless, the brief but dynamic intervening period, bracketed by the demise of formal engraving and the emergence of inexpensive photographic technologies, saw the rise of ethnic caricature as a representational technique in both literature and journalistic art. The surprising nature of this collaboration has provided a focus for my inquiries into the work of major American realists, including Twain, James, Wharton, Chesnutt, and, of course, William Dean Howells, to whose career I now turn.

I

William Dean Howells
and the Touch of Exaggeration
That Typifies

In one of the most famous sallies of the "realism war," Howells imagines how a wretchedly sophisticated pedant might address an entomologist:

> I see that you are looking at a grasshopper there which you have found in the grass, and I suppose you intend to describe it. Now don't waste your time and sin against culture in that way. I've got a grasshopper here, which has been evolved at considerable pains and expense out of the grasshopper in general; in fact, it's a type. . . . It isn't very much like a real grasshopper, but it's a great deal nicer, and it's served to represent the notion of a grasshopper ever since man emerged from barbarism.[1]

With good-natured disdain, Howells suggests that the pedant's arrogant commitment to "type" is itself an unacknowledged vestige of barbarism, and he looks forward to an era when such people and their corrupt sensibilities "must die out" and give "the simple, honest, and natural grasshopper . . . a fair field" (301). He makes clear that in literature as in science the future belongs to the realist, whose method begins with the repudiation of "type."

This account of an evolutionary process governing the development of representational practices underlies Howells's assessment of individual writers as well. Balzac earns praise for his panoramic vision of nineteenth-century society, but he cannot resist "the touch of exaggeration which typifies" (303). The great French novelist possesses the wholesome instincts of a realist, but "Balzac lived too soon to profit by Balzac," and thus he too often yields to a "primitive and inevitable" impulse "to surcharge his characters." The "true realist," Howells explains, knows instinctively that "no living man is a type, but a character." Thus Balzac's naive and imperfect method suffers by comparison with "the later men," who "let characters suffice for themselves" (303).

Another of Howells's favorite writers, Thackeray, betrays the same "toxic" susceptibility to the excesses of type. Returning to *Vanity Fair* as a middle-aged critic, Howells finds the novel "crude, heavy-handed, caricatured," and he marvels at the passion he felt for Thackeray's fiction as a boy, a passion he now regards "almost as a moral defect."[2] From *The Irish Sketchbook* to *Henry Esmond,* Thackeray's fictional world appears grossly "overcolored" to Howells's mature critical vision, and he rationalizes his adolescent fascination with the Englishman's "prodigious works of art" by reasoning that caricature itself is the expression of a childlike, primitive imaginative faculty. Like Balzac, the author of *Pendennis* and *Barry Lyndon* lived too soon to profit from his own example, for "it was the vice of Thackeray, or of Thackeray's time, to surcharge all imitations of life and character, so that a generation apparently much slower if not duller than ours, should not possibly miss the artist's meaning."[3]

Dickens provides yet another dubious example in Howells's evolutionary scheme. Although he surpasses his contemporaries in attending to the details of everyday life, Dickens betrays his primitivism by allowing incident, rather than character, to fuel the engine of his fiction. "The true plot," Howells counsels, "comes out of character; that is, the man does not result from the things he does, but the things he does result from the man."[4] As neither Balzac nor Thackeray, much less Dickens, was capable of understanding, "character" is the appropriate subject of any mature attempt to represent reality. Howells points to Henry James as the writer most likely to be celebrated by future generations, for his neglect of "storytelling" appeals to an emerging "philosophic desire" among readers interested exclusively in the reality of "character."[5] "Plot afterthought does not characterize," Howells concludes; "Dickens thought it did."[6]

As the persistence of this critical strategy implies, the terms "character" and "type" form a crucial opposition in Howells's thinking about literary representation, and he uses these terms to evoke a broad range of concerns. Character identifies a fictional device that Howells prefers to emphasize over plot or story—character, that is, in the sense of a fictional personage—but the term also operates in a psychological register, where it denotes personal integrity or moral fiber. Howells allows these meanings to overlap everywhere in his critical prose, so that his advice to writers ("true plot comes out of character") gestures toward both a literary aesthetic and a corresponding theory of identity. The legitimate subject of any representational act, from the description of a grasshopper to Balzac's expansive *Comedie Humaine,* according to Howells, is character, for character is the raw material of identity, the essential stuff of which the "self" or "personality" is a momentary expression. Howells's conviction that "the man does not result from the things he does, but the things he does result from the man" assumes the existence of a solid core of identity, a foundation that may be articulated outwardly through actions, but that exists prior to any effort at self-expression. Balzac, Thackeray, and Dickens fail the realist litmus test because each in his own way obscures or distorts this foundational account of identity, allowing character to appear unhinged from its essential source. Rather than take up the question of identity in earnest, all three writers "surcharge" their fictional people by indulging what Howells considers a primitive appetite for the abstractions of "type."

Character remains a slippery term in Howells's critical thinking, however, and its serious study produces another sort of abstraction. Dismissing the pedant's misguided advice, the entomologist in Howells's abbreviated drama presumably turns his attention to "the simple, honest, and natural grasshopper" in an effort to learn something about the character of grasshoppers. If his research is successful, he will draw conclusions about the grasshopper in general, conclusions that differ from the pedant's in that they are based on careful observation, but that are reached by a similar process of inference. Howells employs this process of inference himself when he speculates that the essence of character, the proper object of realist analysis in fiction, is the same in everyone, regardless of superficial economic, cultural, or physiognomic qualities that ostensibly differentiate the types of mankind. Some people may have more of it than others, some may have forgotten they ever had it, but we all possess a measure of character, and it is the same essential substance in each of us. Transcending temporal barriers of class, ethnicity, and culture, character links every individual to an abstractly conceived universal human community, and Howells's "true realist" is the artist who affirms this fundamental belief. "Human nature is the same in all environments," he explains, "and the chief delight that an author can give the reader is the delight of discovering it the same under all the masks and disguises that novel conditions have put upon it; of finding himself, his motives, principles, passions reflected in people of a wholly different tradition and physiognomy. This perpetually fascinates and perpetually satisfies; this forms the solidarity of all the arts, and the universality of fiction, which is the highest of the arts."[7]

Realism's concentrated focus on character in its local conditions—the "simple, honest, and natural" human subject—offers Howells's late nineteenth-century readers the chance to gaze through the confusion of present social conditions in order to appreciate "the equality of things and the unity of men."[8] To be a person of character—or to write fiction in which "the characters suffice for themselves"—is to delineate the barely perceptible thread of continuity that unites all humans, for "men are more alike than unalike one another," and the highest office of art is to allow them "to know one another better, that they may be all humbled and strengthened with a sense of their fraternity."[9]

If the moral, political, and aesthetic goal of Howellsian realism is to affirm the solidarity of mankind through the delineation of character, ethnic caricature might be understood as realism's representational antithesis: the language of abstract types. Like romantic fiction, whose "aristocratic spirit" feeds on an immoral "pride of caste," caricature aggressively contests the egalitarian impulse of realism by distorting the essential fraternity of mankind, offering in its place a human menagerie of discrete ethnic identities.[10] Indeed, Howells's evolutionary account of the rise of a realist sensibility in America during the latter half of the nineteenth century is complicated by the simultaneous emergence of an outlandish ethnic iconography, which often competed with realist fiction for space in the nation's leading periodicals. At the height of Howells's critical influence, as he preached the virtues of "democracy in literature" from the "Editor's Study" at *Harper's,* an adjacent column entitled the "Editor's Drawer" regularly featured comic images of various ethnic and cultural types (figure 1.1).[11] Literary and graphic caricaturists of the period delighted in confounding the vision of an assimilated United States, not to mention a universal fraternity of man, by revealing that ethnic characteristics—what Howells would call "the masks and disguises that novel conditions have put upon" identity—are permanently inscribed in nature. When Mr. Cohn marries Miss O'Rourke in a typical *Puck* cartoon, their hybrid American offspring in no way escapes the physical stigma of ethnic origin. Exaggerated racial markers are merely compounded in *Puck's* illustration of the second generation Jewish-Irish immigrant, in whom ethnic type forms the unalloyed basis of identity (figure 1.2).

Howells's impatience with such divisive "humor" is unquestionably sincere. In condemning the excesses of Thackeray's art, he can

FIGURE 1.1. "Editor's Drawer," *Harper's Monthly* 77 (August 1888): 319.

FIGURE 1.2. "Hereditary Types," *Puck*, date unknown, reproduced in John J. Appel, "Jews in American Caricature: 1820–1914," *American Jewish History* 71 (September 1981): 132.

think of no more derogatory term than "caricature" to describe what he considers an inferior brand of fiction.[12] But just as *Harper's* permitted odd juxtapositions of realism and caricature within its consistently middle-brow pages, Howells comes strangely close to employing the technique of ethnic caricature in the act of repudiating its use. Indeed, one imagines that Balzac, given the chance to answer Howells's assessment of the *Comedie Humaine*, might have object that the "savages" and "barbarians" who serve throughout the "Criticism and Fiction" as representatives of an uncivilized critical disposition are themselves "surcharged" with "the touch of exaggeration which typifies." In describing these unnamed proletarians, who prefer "burlesque and negro minstrelsy" to realist character analysis, Howells creates a vivid picture of urban savagery, drawing freely on Wild West imagery to characterize—or caricature—his unnamed opponents in the realism war.[13] "Many persons in every civilized community live in a state of more or less evident savagery," he explains with qualified sympathy, "and they are held in check only by the law" (330). Such aesthetic degenerates are "savage in their tastes," which resemble the unregulated appetites of "a boy of thirteen or a barbarian of any age." Apparently forgetting his antipathy for the language of types, Howells frequently deploys this modified logic of ethnic caricature in defense of realism, as when he describes the "stock hero" of popular fiction as "really a painted barbarian, the prey of his passions and delusions, full of obsolete ideals, and the motives and ethics of a savage" (326). As the invective against popular forms of entertainment reaches an elevated pitch, Howells's defensive imagery draws more and more insistently from the repertoire of the ethnic caricaturist, and, as a paradoxical consequence, the tone of the "Editor's Study" becomes almost indistinguishable from that of the "Editor's Drawer."

The terms of Howells's bipolar analysis—realism and caricature, character and type—again overlap unpredictably in his call for a fiction of "true proportions." Impatient with the gross distortions that pass for "art" among the uncivilized masses, Howells declares: "[L]et fiction cease to lie about life; . . . let it leave off painting dolls and working them by springs and wires; . . . let it speak the dialect, the language, that most Americans know—the language of unaffected people everywhere" (328). As a lingua franca for the common man, dialect, according to this appeal, is consistent with the official social vision of realism. Howells famously championed many of the most controversial dialect writers of the period, including Stephen

Crane and Hamlin Garland, and he advocated its use in fiction as a matter of aesthetic and political principle, arguing that familiarity with regional linguistic idiosyncrasies would promote a spirit of national unity.

Yet in practice this "language of unaffected people everywhere" often serves to emphasize the utter strangeness of unassimilable elements within what Basil March calls "our heterogeneous commonwealth."[14] As March contemplates the "unintelligible dialect" of Italian workers in *A Hazard of New Fortunes,* he poses a "question within himself as to what notion these poor animals formed of a free republic from their experience of life under its conditions" (182). March's physical proximity to these "beasts" is one effect of the elevated railway's "erasing line," which throws New Yorkers of every class together into an unprecedented social context, forcing March to acknowledge the "numerical subordination of the dominant race" throughout the city (183). New York's unintelligible dialects become one means of restoring this tenuous line between respectability and barbarism. Dialect, in other words, performs the social work of caricature, fixing identity according to discrete and inflexible ethnic characteristics. March's keen ear and sharp eye allow him to categorize New York's ethnic types according to the same phonetic and physiognomic cliches that were standard fare in magazines such as *Harper's Monthly* and, one suspects, March's own *Every Other Week:* "the small eyes, the high cheeks, the broad noses, the puff lips, the bare, cue-fitted skulls, of Russians, Poles, Czechs, Chinese; the furtive glitter of Italians; the blond dullness of Germans; the cold quiet of Scandinavians—fire under ice—were aspects that he identified and that gave him abundant suggestion . . . for the more public-spirited reveries in which he dealt with the future economy of our heterogeneous commonwealth" (183).

The thick German accent of *Hazard's* most compelling dialect speaker, Lindau, suggests the same paradoxical overlap between realist principle and the technique of caricature. As a literary scholar, socialist, and freedom fighter, Lindau articulates Howells's profound belief in the underlying equality of human beings. In conversation with March, he defends the rights of the poor and disadvantaged, employing his native language to attack "the landlords and the merchant princes, the railroad kings and the coal barons" who "gather their millions together from the hunger and cold and despair of hundreds of thousands of other men" (191). Lindau's dialect might logically function as the linguistic extension of his socialist vision, a

language of the common man, whose stylistic resources would promote unity among workers, immigrants, and other victims of urban
poverty.

But Lindau's broken English has precisely the opposite effect.
When March rises to leave, alarmed at the radical tone of the old
man's German speech, Lindau "suddenly broke into a laugh and into
English. 'Oh, well, it is only dalk, Passil, and it toes me goodt. My
parg is worse then my pidte, I cuess" (193). Laughter is the appropriate
accompaniment to Lindau's immigrant English, for both he and
Howells employ this highly idiosyncratic language to temper the
"pidte" of Lindau's ideology, clothing his revolutionary ideas in a
ridiculous idiom that transforms "poor" to "boor," "principles" to
"brincibles," "capital" to "gabidal," and so on. Dialect here is a mask-
ing device that allows Howells to import socialist thinking into the
novel, while ensuring that Lindau's ideas remain linguistically mar-
ginalized at the ethnic periphery of March's consciousness. Far from
extending the bonds of sympathy to include members of New York's
burgeoning "other half" in an inclusive social vision—a vision sanc-
tioned by Howellsian realism—Lindau's comic pronunciation only
confirms his status as an irreparable alien, a caricature of the beer-
drinking German intellectual who possesses more passion than common sense (figure 1.3).[15] The "old dynamiter," as Fulkerson calls him,
paradoxically expresses realism's profoundest social aspirations, even
as his caricatured image makes those aspirations ridiculous (145).

My point is not that Howells defaults on his commitment to an
inclusive literary aesthetic, a "language of unaffected people everywhere," when he deploys the stigma of ethnic dialect. Elsa Nettles,
who has written more insightfully on this question than any other
critic, takes a hard line on such apparent lapses, maintaining that
"whenever dialect in Howells's fiction reinforces a racial stereotype, it
violates two of his principles of realism: that human nature is essentially the same in all times and places and that human character is
not fixed but variable."[16] Critics have generally accepted some version of this reasonable judgment, which understands Howells's curious resort to caricature in the representation of ethnic subjects as a
lapse in his otherwise sound commitment to realist principle. But
such a view underrates the complexity and persistence of his engagement with the logic of types. Howells does not simply lose sight of
realism's social objectives—its commitment to "character"—in his
treatment of ethnic identity, nor is he naive about the limiting force
of ethnic stigmas, such as Lindau's dialect or the "cue-fitting skulls of

A LOST OPPORTUNITY.

FIRST COMMUNIST.—"Tell you what 'tis, cit'zen Schmidt, this here American people ain't got no enterprise—no snap—not sense enough to know a good chance when they see it. Why, this here election was jest bilin' over with a good show for anarchy—an' did they take it up? No, sirree."

SECOND CHILD OF PROGRESS.—"Nah! Dot vos so. Dere vosn't aenarchy enough in 'em to prake a beer-zaloon open, ain't it? I shame myself for dot holy banner of communismus, my frent. Uf some of dem colletch shtudents don't choin us, ve vos up der shpout gegone, dot's sairtin."

FIGURE 1.3. F. Graetz, "A Lost Opportunity," *Puck* 10 (December 3, 1884): 214.

Russians, Poles, Czechs, Chinese." Rather, we need only recall the painted barbarians of "Criticism and Fiction" to appreciate that Howells consistently deploys the technique of ethnic caricature to articulate realism's ambivalent repudiation of type. A more provocative way of making the same point would be to suggest that Howellsian realism institutes permanent and inflexible ethnic and cultural categories as a strategy for imagining a homogeneous social order.

This conceptual slight-of-hand is a basic maneuver in realist fiction, and other writers were equally effective at having it both ways with the art of caricature. Henry James, to name one, was prone to follow Howells in identifying caricature as an impoverished representational mode, even as he portrayed the impulse to *employ* caricature as a fundamental expression of realist sensibility. The paradox is evident when Mr. Touchett in *The Portrait of a Lady* remarks that a lady novelist once "published a work of fiction in which she was understood to have given a representation—something in the nature of a caricature, as you might say—of my unworthy self."[17] The old man is willing to see his "American peculiarities, nasal twang, [and] Yankee notions" adapted to fiction, but he complains that the mode of caricature recklessly distorts reality: "I had no objection to her giving a report of my conversation, if she liked; but I didn't like the idea that she hadn't taken the trouble to listen to it." Caricature fails to provide an accurate account of Mr. Touchett's brisk utilitarian idiom, and yet James elsewhere treats the impulse to deploy carica-ture as a technique for effectively managing one's relationships with potentially enthralling elements in the social world. Thus Ralph Touchett expresses sincere affection for his cousin a few pages after this scene when he playfully draws "a caricature of her in which she was represented as a very pretty young woman dressed . . . in the folds of the national banner."[18] This image is no more accurate than the unnamed woman novelist's literary caricature of Mr. Touchett, and yet Ralph's mode of representing Isabel's nationalistic charm signifies his recognition of her naive political passion. Caricature here connotes a healthy ocular detachment, something Ralph soon loses—with serious consequences for himself and for Isabel—when he begins to regard her instead as "finer than the finest work of art."[19]

Howells is even more deliberate than James in treating the im-pulse to caricature as evidence of a well-adjusted critical vision. Bromfield Corey explicitly lacks this vision when he struggles unsuc-cessfully to understand what his son admires about the "rude, native flavor" of Silas Lapham.[20] As Phillip Barrish has explained, Corey labors to make Lapham's boorishness palatable by imbuing the old man's image with "poetry" and "romance" (920). Howells mocks this effort to render Lapham's crude ways "exotically picturesque," an ef-fort he portrays as, according to Barrish, "a form of cultural . . . benightedness that is inseparable from aesthetic laziness."[21]

In contrast to his father's picturesque maneuvers, Tom Corey re-sponds to Lapham's roughness with a blend of identification and condescension: "I 'took to' Colonel Lapham from the moment I saw him," he explains to his father. "He looked as if he 'meant business,' and I mean business too" (921). As Barrish explains, "Silas and business have a one-to-one relation," such that the proposition "he 'meant business'" can be taken literally as a caricatured representa-tion of the single-minded rustic capitalist: Lapham is another word for business. Moreover, the internal quotation marks indicate that although Tom quotes Lapham's vernacular idiom approvingly, he is careful to avoid "unselfconsciously merging it with his own" more refined style of speaking.[22] In drawing on the power of Lapham's vulgarity without being limited by it, Tom identifies himself with what Howells understands as a privileged sensibility: unlike his father, he grasps the force of Lapham's dialect, and yet unlike members of Lapham's own family (with the exception of Penelope), he recognizes the old man's colloquialisms as marking the limited intellectual horizon of a rustic type. Whereas Bromfield Corey's picturesque image misconstrues the common man as something acceptable to genteel tastes, Tom's mode of caricature appreciates Lapham's vulgarity as a source of energy, even as it shelters Tom's investment in taste-values that closely resemble those of his father. Caricature—or, as Barrish eloquently puts it, the ability "to take quiet pleasure in the exercise of 'crude' taste"—emerges as a privileged form of representation, one that distinguishes Tom from the corrupt aestheticism of his father and identifies him instead with the ostensibly progressive imperatives of Howellsian realism.[23]

Howells's protagonists repeatedly make this move, despite his professed misgivings about caricature as an inferior or childlike mode or representation. Basil March is perhaps literary realism's most notorious caricaturist, but Ben Halleck in *A Modern Instance,* Reverend Sewell in *The Minister's Charge,* and Dr. Olney in *An Imperative Duty,* to name only a few of the most obvious cases, all assert a privileged sensibility by viewing *others* through the lens of caricature. In fact, this view becomes almost a reflex whenever Howells introduces rustic, single-minded, or otherwise one-dimensional characters into his fiction. Lindau's passionate advocacy of the poor blinds him to any conception of social justice other than the one he espouses, just as the elder Mr. Dryfoos can approach ethical questions only from the point of view of big business. In their extreme commitment to a single account of truth or fairness, such characters make themselves "the easy prey of caricature," as Howells puts it elsewhere, and Basil March earns important realist credentials by seizing this prey at every opportunity in *A Hazard of New Fortunes.*[24] In fact, Howellsian realism never commits itself to an identifiable moral or political vision. The sensibility privileged over and over in his fiction is one capable of recognizing the limitation of any view of reality that forecloses some other view of reality, a sensibility capable of finding both Lindau and Dryfoos partly right and partly ridiculous. Basil March, like Halleck, Sewell, and many of Howells's other decidedly unheroic protagonists, asserts his claim to this privileged vantage by practicing the art of caricature—by demonstrating, in other words, that figures such as Lindau and Dryfoos are reducible to a single idea, whereas the Howellsian realist operates in multiple cultural registers at once.

If I am right that the ability to delineate one-dimensionality serves as a meaningful credential of realist sensibility within Howells's fiction, then it should come as no surprise that for all his commitment to "character," Howells's novels include many figures who prove themselves "the easy prey of caricature." This oddly dependent relationship between seemingly antithetical modes of representation—one that might be called *realist character analysis,* another that Howells typically identifies as *mere caricature*—is especially apparent in his first-person sketches of urban life. Registering profound discomfort at "the encroachment of the Celtic army" in "A Pedestrian Tour," for example, Howells adopts the alarmist tone of more reactionary observers, such as Madison Grant and Lothrop Stoddard, predicting "an end of us poor Yankees as a dominant plurality."[25] The elder race of Americans who once inhabited the present Irish neighborhoods of Boston, "a population now as extinct in that region as the Pequots," has been replaced not by a new kind of American citizen but by an impersonal ethnic and cultural force, "something that takes the wrong side, as by instinct, in politics; something that mainly helps to prop up tottering priestcraft among us; something that one thinks of with dismay as destined to control so largely the civil and religious interests of the country" (69–70).

Metaphors of "infection" and "siege" further dehumanize the subjects of Howells's pedestrian analysis, which culminates in the frightening image of an immigrant vice grip. Speaking for a disappearing race of Yankees, the narrator is resigned to await "with an anxious curiosity the encounter of the Irish and the Chinese, now rapidly approaching each other from opposite shores of the continent. Shall we be crushed in the collision of these superior races? Every intelligence-office will soon be ringing with the cries of combat, and all our kitchens strewn with pig-tails and bark chignons" (71–72).

The unmistakable element of ethnic caricature in this fanciful image of combat between domestic servants intends to allay nativist anxiety in the act of expressing it, reminding "us poor Yankees" that the "superior races" promise to become superior in numbers only. The sketch plays heavily on standard cultural clichés that serve to legitimize Yankee hegemony, as when the narrator declares that in every Irish shop "you doubtless find a lady before the counter in the act of putting down a guilty-looking tumbler with one hand, while she neatly wipes her mouth on the back of the other" (67). Such aggressive typification leads Howells to arrive at the conclusion generally reached by his counterparts in the graphic departments at both *Harper's* and *Puck:* namely, that Boston's Irish-Americans are fundamentally Irish, not American, and that no amount of cultural mimicry can erase "the difference that must exist between a race immemorially civilized and one which has lately emerged from barbarism" (66) (figure 1.4).

These are surprising attitudes in a writer who understands that "no living man is a type, but a character," and Howells has been duly criticized in his own time and ours for his failure to apply the aesthetic standards of realism in his representation of ethnic figures.[26] Yet to dismiss such anomalous moments in Howells's work as methodological inconsistencies or lapses in technique is to overlook the important role of nativism as an element in Howells's thinking

POOR PAT'S PERSECUTORS.

THE IRISH LEECHES AND THEIR VICTIM.

FIGURE 1.4. Frederick Opper, "Poor Pat's Persecutors: The Irish Leeches and Their Victim," *Puck,* March 7, 1883.

about character, identity, and citizenship. In fact, if we contain our discomfort with the ethnic chauvinism of "A Pedestrian Tour" long enough to consider the sketch fully, it becomes plain that Howells's effort to combat nativist anxiety introduces its own difficulties. Simply put, if the Irishman *is* reducible to certain physiognomic cues and a set of ethnically specific tendencies toward drunkenness, priestcraft, and political conspiracy, then there is no common source of identity, no transethnic reservoir of "character" underlying human diversity and grounding identity in a shared foundation. This is a far more terrifying prospect for Howells than the "advent of the Irish," that "calamitous race," into Boston's once respectable neighborhoods (71). Ethnic caricature may quell one set of anxieties, but it feeds a more profound concern about the nature of identity and the potential for sympathy among humans. In typically ambivalent fashion, Howells addresses this larger worry through his image of "Mrs. Clannahan," a fictitious Irish housewife who resembles the standard magazine figures "Paddy" and "Bridget" in being less an individual than a proper name that stands for a cultural idea. "Mrs. Clannahan's kitchen, as it may be seen by the desperate philosopher when he goes to engage her for the spring house-cleaning, is a strong argument against his fears. If Mrs. Clannahan, lately of an Irish cabin, can show a kitchen so capably appointed and so neatly kept as that, the country may yet be an inch or two from the brink of ruin, and the race which we trust as little as we love may turn out no more spendthrift than most heirs" (70).

Mrs. Clannahan is little more than a cartoon figure, a stock representative of her menial race, and the "desperate philosopher" is significantly not so desperate that he must encounter her as anything but a domestic servant. But the passage does not follow through on this comfortingly hierarchical arrangement of types, for Mrs. Clannahan's kitchen is an argument against the philosopher's nativist fears and against ethnic caricature as a technique for allaying those fears. "We must make a jest of our own alarms, and even smile," Howells later concedes, for the physical and cultural attributes that appear to differentiate the Irish as a separate and inferior race, attributes that are deliberately exaggerated even here, may represent no difference at all. These two quite incompatible impulses—one that conceives of the Irish servant as a racial type, another that questions the logic of typification—are in fact complementary and mutually enabling features of Howells's realist practice.

"A Pedestrian Tour" appeared in Howells's 1871 *Suburban*

Sketches. The following year James R. Osgood published an illustrated edition, whose cover featured the image of an African-American child, "Naomi," executed by Augustus Hoppin in strict conformity with the period's conventions of "coon" caricature (figure 1.5). Much like Stowe's Topsy in *Uncle Tom's Cabin*, the 1852 novel that established many late nineteenth-century norms for the representation of African-American "character," Naomi's kinky hair and mischievous grin—what Howells calls her "ragged gayety" in the sketch entitled "Mrs. Johnson"—denote a strain of "summer in the blood" (20).[27] Indeed, Hoppin's engraving directly anticipates E. W. Kemble's conception of the irrepressible Topsy in Houghton Mifflin's 1896 reissue of *Uncle Tom's Cabin,* an edition that curiously weds the rhetoric of abolition with that of "coon" era racist iconography. Howells adds an element of exoticism to Stowe's representation of the "pickaninny" type by explaining that Naomi and her mother, Mrs. Johnson, were "doubly estranged by descent," for "a sylvan wildness mixed with that of the desert" in their veins. Mrs. Johnson's grandfather "was an Indian," according to the narrator, "and her ancestors on this side had

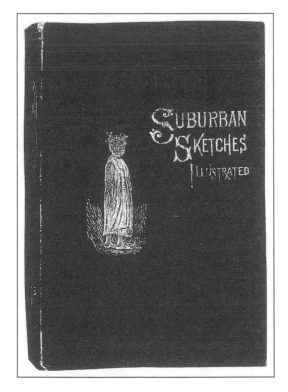

FIGURE 1.5. Augustus Hoppin, cover illustration for *Suburban Sketches* (Boston: James R. Osgood, 1872).

probably sold their lands for the same value in trinkets that bought the original African pair on the other side" (21).

Howells deploys these ethnic categories with little subtlety, attributing Naomi's aboriginal streak of independence to her "sylvan blood," whereas the girl's African heritage accounts for the intellectual limitations that render her powerless as a reader "before words of one syllable" (27–28). Such fine genealogical distinctions between "the Indian's hauteur" and "the Ethiope's . . . abundant amiability" coincide in the generalized image of a primitive sensibility, characterized by obsessive fondness for shiny objects and an irrepressibly emotional constitution. Without a trace of New England "conscience" to deepen their simple natures, the ethnic primitives of Howells's sketch are defined by a set of rigidly conventional traits, as Hoppin emphasizes in his illustration of the massive, genderless, turbaned Mrs. Johnson, enjoying her evening pipe (figure 1.6). A parallel illustration from George A. Thompson's *Coonah Town Sassiety* confirms that the visual cues that constitute Mrs. Johnson's identity in both picture and text serve less to characterize than to typify her image (figure 1.7). An inflexible link between physiognomy and ethnic identity is further emphasized when Howells adds another detail from the lexicon of contemporary "coon" humor, explaining that Mrs. Johnson's son-in-law is a professor of phrenology, who is "believed to have uncommon virtue in his science by reason of being blind as well as black" (24).

Playing hard and fast with such an array of ethnic identifiers, the first-person narrator of "Mrs. Johnson" is amused at African-American efforts "to assume something of our race's colder demeanor," but he is "better pleased when they forget us, and ungenteelly laugh in encountering friends, letting their white teeth glitter through the generous lips that open to their ears" (19). Magazine images of the period constantly enacted this spectacle of failed imitation, in which black figures attempt pathetically to engage in middle-class behavior, despite manifest physiognomic "evidence" of their barbaric or subhuman origins (figure 1.8). Howells's sketch turns on a similar comic assumption, allowing Mrs. Johnson's naive social aspirations to reinforce the narrator's powerful sense of estrangement from the dark-skinned people who live in "indolent oblivion in their quarter of the city" (18).

But the aggressively demeaning logic of ethnic caricature serves to estrange Mrs. Johnson only in order to emphasize the unaccountable depth of her "character" in the sketch's emotional closing scene.

FIGURE 1.6. Augustus Hoppin, "She Lighted a Potent Pipe," frontispiece for *Suburban Sketches* (Boston: James R. Osgood, 1872).

FIGURE 1.7. George A. Thompson, *Coonah Town Sassiety and Other Comic Stories in Picture and Rhyme* (Chicago: Laird & Lee, 1903).

FIGURE 1.8. E. W. Kemble, *The Adventures of the Blackberries* (New York: R. H. Russell, 1897).

Unlike Jenny, the Irish girl who abandons the narrator's kitchen without a second thought in the sketch's opening scene, Mrs. Johnson struggles with complex emotions when she is forced to choose between rival obligations to her family and to her employers. Howells invests her quaint dialect with a sentimental rather than comic tone, as she delivers the sketch's final speech: "I hope I ha'n't put you out any. I *wanted* to go with you, but I ought to *knowed* I couldn't. All is, I loved you too much" (34). Traces of the Plantation Tradition are audible in this affectionate climax, which does nothing to rescue Mrs. Johnson's image from the grip of convention. Yet in declaring her love for her employers—a love that is clearly reciprocated—she upsets the narrator's comfortable impression of an unbridgeable "gulf" between the menial and the dominant races, forcing him to reconsider the space of difference that his ethnic imagery has sustained, and that his neatly stratified view of the social world requires. As usual, Howells wears his ambivalence on his sleeve when he allows his narrator to admit that "[i]t was only her barbaric laughter and her lawless eye that betrayed how slightly her New England birth and breeding covered her ancestral traits, and bridged the gulf of a thousand years of civilization that lay between her race and ours" (20–21).

This passage might serve as a model for Howells's approach to the representation of ethnic identity, for it both asserts a permanent gulf between the "higher" and "lower" races and bridges that gulf by declaring that it was *only* Mrs. Johnson's laugher and facial expression, contingent rather than essential aspects of her identity, that "betrayed" her barbaric origin. Only by having it both ways—by claiming Mrs. Johnson as an equal in everything that matters, while demonstrating her fundamental inferiority—can Howells finesse his own precarious social situation in the *Suburban Sketches*. It is not that he shuttles unpredictably between the representational priorities of the realist and those of the caricaturist, for as in the image of Mrs. Clannahan Howells manages to typify and to characterize his subject simultaneously. Mrs. Johnson both underwrites a hopeful conception of human fraternity and allays nativist fears about racial imposture and usurpation, establishing a zone of security in which the realist writer can imagine a richly heterogeneous social world that is perfectly free of class and ethnic conflict.[28]

In referring to Howells's ambivalence, I do not mean to suggest that he is either confused or duplicitous when he performs this double movement. Indeed, the same paradox of estrangement and identification that complicates the narrator's representation of African Americans in "Mrs. Johnson" also informs *her* attitude toward her white employers, as the narrator is amused to acknowledge. Subscribing to the views of her late husband, who had "written a book to show the superiority of the black over the white branches of the human family," Mrs. Johnson maintains an unflattering view of "the Caucasian Race," whom she considers "an upstart people of new blood, who had come by their whiteness by no creditable or pleasant process" (24). For all her "very good philosophical and Scriptural" arguments in defense of black superiority, however, Mrs. Johnson refuses to attend church "with people of her elder and wholesomer blood" and insists on a "remarkable approach to whiteness in many of her own offspring" (25–26). These efforts to construct a racial hierarchy, while at the same time transgressing its leading assumptions about racial difference, strike the narrator as mildly tragic, but he acknowledges that his own representational practice involves the same internal contradiction. Speculating on the sources of the old woman's "original and suggestive" imagination, he admits that "we were perhaps too fond of explaining its peculiarities by facts of

ancestry,—of finding hints of the Powwow or the Grand Custom
in each grotesque development. We were conscious of something
warmer in this old soul than in ourselves, and something wilder, and
we chose to think it the tropic and the untracked forest" (29).

In identifying his mode of characterization as a *choice,* the narrator provisionally liberates his image of Mrs. Johnson from the "facts
of ancestry" that appear to explain "each grotesque development" of
her identity. The move is made consciously and deliberately as a
counterpoint to the narrator's otherwise perfect adherence to the
conventions of ethnic caricature. Something similar happens in "An
East-Side Ramble," where Howells is surprised to discover that Jews
living in the squalor of New York's "Hebrew quarter" are "so like
other human beings and really so little different from the best, except in their environment, that I had to get away from this before
I could regard them as wild beasts."29 The resort to caricature
here and in "Mrs. Johnson" is a conscious choice that restores the
speaker's sense of racial privilege, even as it calls attention to the dubious legitimacy of that privilege.

The narrator of *Suburban Sketches* draws little distinction between the various forms of alienism represented by the Irish and the
Chinese, except to note that they encroach upon New England from
different directions. Mrs. Johnson and Mrs. Clannahan are similarly
interchangeable figures for an ethnic presence that Howells represents with various hues, but with the same thick brush strokes in
each instance. His management of ethnic "types" is more nuanced in
An Imperative Duty, Howells's only extended fictional treatment of
race, and a novel that offers rare insight into the multiple functions
of ethnic caricature within the context of Howellsian realism. Wan-
dering through his native Boston for the first time since his long
residence in Italy, Olney, the white nerve specialist and hero of *An
Imperative Duty,* notes the "bewilderingly strange" social atmosphere
of the city's white neighborhoods, which he attributes to "the curious similarity in the figures and faces of the crowd."30 Further speculation leads Olney to observe "an approach from all directions to a
common type among those who work with their hands for a living;
what he had seen in Liverpool and now saw in Boston was not the
English type or the American type, but the proletarian type" (4).

This flattening of cultural and physiognomic diversity is unnerving to Olney, whose financial misfortunes have landed him in a
dingy boardinghouse in an unfashionable part of town. Eager to differentiate his own questionable social status from that of an emerg-

ing proletarian class, he takes comfort in observing that the older Irish women still possess "the simian cast of features which affords the caricaturist such an unmistakable Irish physiognomy."[31] But the "secondary Irish," especially the young women, betray distressingly few traits of ethnic origin, leading Olney to theorize reluctantly that "if they survive to be mothers they may give us, with better conditions, a race as hale and handsome as the elder American race" (4).

This is unquestionably a version of the Howellsian ethnic two-step, a conceptual dance around the issue of ethnic identity that understands the Irish paradoxically as both "simian" and nominally "American." Olney strains to dismantle the paradox, for his tenuous claim to social distinction depends on his ability to communicate his privileged status decisively and unambiguously. The ubiquitous Irish confound his efforts at differentiation by dressing themselves with ridiculous formality, and even the "unmistakable Irish physiognomy" fails as a reliable guarantee of the privileges associated with "authentic" citizenship. Thus to reclaim some measure of social prestige in the ethnic flux of the modern city, Olney becomes a caricaturist himself, noting the "hairy paw" thrust forward by an aggressive Irish waiter as a metonym for the ape-like race whose representatives hover around his table in search of tips (5). The Irish are literally and figuratively too close for Olney's comfort, and no amount of dehumanizing imagery appears sufficient to shield his nativist anxieties from the sensation, as he contemplates his dinner, of warm Irish breath "coming and going on the bald spot on his crown" (5).

Olney's elaborate emotional response to the Irish presence in his former home contrasts sharply with his impression of Boston's African Americans. Blacks differ from "every other sort of aliens" he encounters in that nothing in their adopted Yankee environment serves to "characterize their manner" (6). Unlike the pushy Irish, who are constantly threatening to become indistinguishable from "Americans," black Bostonians have the decency and "tact" to remain perfectly outside Olney's privileged sphere, and thus he idealizes their "shining . . . good-nature and good-will" as a model of virtuous alienism (6–7). What strikes Olney as "altogether agreeable" about African Americans, in contrast with the rest of "our mixed humanity," is the willingness "of colored people to keep to themselves in all public places." "They were just as free to come to the music on the Common that Sunday afternoon as any of the white people he saw there. . . . But he found very few of them there" (6).

Clearly what appeals to Olney about African Americans is their willingness to be absent from his troubled impressions, a willingness that paradoxically stimulates his desire for more contact and leads, by a circuitous route, to the novel's miscegenation plot. Yet even when African Americans occupy Olney's impressions with something more substantial than their absence, they gratify his nativist impulse by adopting the conventional personae familiar to ethnic caricaturists of the period. A black waiter might be as greedy at heart as an Irish one, Olney speculates, but the African American "would have clothed his greed in such a smiling courtesy and such a childish simple-heartedness that it would have been graceful and winning" (5). Although he recognizes this act of self-representation as a calculated performance, Olney takes obvious comfort in the black waiter's willingness to "clothe" himself in a costume that leaves no uncertainty about the nerve specialist's right to a privileged social status.

More than social status is at stake, however, in this self-conscious enactment of a cultural role, and Olney's strong attraction to the novel's African-American figures emerges from a more profound form of interest in the spectacle of reified ethnic performance. Indeed, Boston's African Americans present themselves to the nerve specialist's troubled nativist vision as not only "clothed" to appease his anxieties, but "clothed through and through," literally constituted by their clothing. Fascinated by the uncanny impression of weightlessness and insubstantiality displayed by a group of "very effective dandies of the type we were then beginning to call dude," he contemplates the "ultra-correctness" of their appearance, and goes on to observe that "they had that air of being clothed through and through, as to the immortal spirit as well as the perishable body, by their cloth gaiters, their light trousers, their neatly buttoned cutaway coats, their harmonious scarfs, and their silk hats" (7).

To be "clothed through and through," as Howells would be the first to explain, is to lack "character," the foundation upon which identity presumably rests. In their exaggerated conformity to the "type" of the African-American "dude" or "swell," a type well known to caricaturists of the day, Olney's black dandies bring this alternative vision of human identity within Howells's reach (figure 1.9). For both Olney and the author, the boldly sketched black figure makes available an enticing taboo, the image of an undifferentiated, fluid, and irresponsible self.

Howells was notoriously squeamish about representing such a model of identity, a free-floating self that—as Henry James might

FIGURE 1.9. George A. Thompson, *Coonah Town Sassiety and Other Comic Stories in Picture and Rhyme* (Chicago: Laird & Lee, 1903).

put it — "overflows into everything," but he was fascinated by the possibilities obscured by this self-imposed limitation.[32] Unable to regulate their appetites and ambitions, Bartley Hubbard in *A Modern Instance* and Angus Beaton in *A Hazard of New Fortunes* exemplify the moral dangers that ensue when the self becomes unhinged from some reliable psychological infrastructure, but Howells typically entertains the image of an untethered consciousness only long enough to explain that its movements take place, as Kaplan explains, "outside the structures of character and beyond the pale of representation."[33] He often explicitly questions the foundations of personality, implying in Beaton's case, for example, that the self is no more than a succession of moods, but this dangerous assertion is treated as "one of those facts which fiction must seek in vain to disclose."[34] In its thorough abstractness, the caricatured African-American image serves Howells as a form of shorthand for the unspeakable possibility of a free-floating self, providing unique access to a psychological condition he can approach only through elaboration of the "coon" image.

Consider, for example, Rhoda Aldgate's chaotic impressions as she wanders through Boston's crowded streets immediately following the revelation of her African-American ancestry. Rhoda initially shares Olney's view that blacks are "burlesques of humanity, worse than apes because they [are] more like," and her impressions carefully register "their flat wide-nostriled noses, their out-rolled thick lips, their mobile, bulging eyes set near together" (58). Prior to the discovery of her ethnic origin, she displays an impressive fluency in the idiom of "coon" caricature, describing a black waiter who is "four feet high," with feet "about eighteen inches long, so that he looks like a capital L." "He doesn't lift them, when he walks," she continues, "but he slips along on them over the floor like a funny little mouse; I've decided to call him Creepy-Mousey: it just exactly describes him, he's so small and cunning" (39). Suddenly coerced into identification with such clownish figures, Rhoda is forced to rethink her own identity in the same terms. This is a catastrophic moment for Rhoda, to say the least, and an exciting one for Howells, who jumps at the chance to get inside a consciousness that is unsupported by the stabilizing force of "character." Without scruple or hesitation, Rhoda's thoughts move rapidly into mental "fastnesses" that are usually closed to Howells's realist practice:

> she seemed to be walking swiftly, flying forward; but the ground was uneven: it rose before her, and then suddenly fell. She felt her heart beat in the middle of her throat. Her head felt light, like the blowball of a dandelion. She wished to laugh. There seemed to be two selves of her, one that had lived before that awful knowledge, and one that had lived as long since, and again a third that knew and pitied them both. She wondered at the same time if this were what people meant by saying one's brain was turned. (60)

There is none of Howells's usual reluctance here about tracing the mental processes of a fractured identity, a self without bearings or substance. Later in the novel, the distorted black image again brings this problematic condition of identity into view when the narrator describes an African-American minister with "no discernible features," who appeared "like a wavering blur against the wall," "entirely black," "a thick, soft shadow" dressed in "absolute sable"

(63). Like the elusive black figures that are palpably absent from the Boston Common, or the ultracorrect dandies who create an impression of unreality, the minister's indistinct form operates for Howells as an emblem of the mind in crisis. As a "wavering blur" clad in "absolute sable," his disembodied image signifies a condition of undifferentiated identity, similar to the condition experienced by Rhoda as she relaxes her control over the movements of consciousness in becoming an ethnic type herself—in this case, until her rescue by an erotically awakened Olney, the type of the "tragic mulatta." Racial caricature functions for Howells as a means to dramatize the eruption into consciousness of psychic possibilities that ought, by design, to remain beyond the realist's representational grasp.[35]

The caricatured African-American image, as I am describing it, signifies a terrifying and, at the same time, compelling form of freedom for Howells, which may explain why his middle-class white characters, including Isabel March in *A Hazard of New Fortunes,* so often declare a perverse "love" for "the whole race" (48).[36] Isabel's surprising enthusiasm for a group of people she knows absolutely nothing about is related to her complicated initiation to New York, a city that "reduces all men to a common level, that touches everybody with its potent magic and brings to the surface the deeply underlying nobody" (243). After "the intense identification of their Boston life," this sacrifice of individuality strikes Isabel as "a relief," though she "had her misgivings, and questioned whether it were not too relaxing to the moral fibre" (297). In response to her equivocation, Basil strikes a characteristically noncommittal Howellsian pose: "March refused to explore his conscience; he allowed that it might be so; but he said he liked now and then to feel his personality in that state of solution" (297).

This intriguing exchange is full of the ambivalence Howells always expresses about the authority of the self and the desirability of its dominion over mental life. He seems tempted to agree with Isabel that the loss of individuality, the emergence of "the deeply underlying nobody," constitutes a relief from the artificial posturing of Boston social life. The narrator goes so far as to say that the effect of New York "for consciousness, for egotism, is admirable" and "doubtless finally wholesome" (243–44). Yet Howells declines to elaborate on this "wholesome" challenge to the self's authority. In keeping with his customary policy, he retreats behind Isabel's "misgivings," offering the disreputable Beaton as the novel's only example of a consciousness unsupported by "moral fibre."

The Marches immediately grasp the moral significance of Beaton's unrestrained consciousness, and the "solvent" quality of New York never reduces them to his level of internal chaos. Nevertheless, Howells does permit Isabel one intriguing moment of unqualified insanity, a moment that occurs in the presence of another curiously abbreviated ethnic figure. "How could I have lost my head so completely?" she asks Basil after almost renting an apartment that meets none of her requirements for cost or comfort (47). Her sudden abandonment of common sense, that all important faculty in Howells's fiction, is provoked by the literally enchanting impression created by "one of those colored men who soften the trade of janitor in many of the smaller apartment-houses in New York by the sweetness of their race" (46). Both the house, with its "dark mahogany trim, of sufficiently ugly design," and the curiously indistinct, "angelic" black janitor, who speaks "winningly" in a thick ethnic dialect, charm Isabel inexplicably (46). The once imposing home of an affluent family is now "cut up into five or six dwellings," an image of the fragmentation March associates with New York, about which Isabel elsewhere expresses an ambiguous blend of "relief" and trepidation (46). Yet her "misgivings" about a weakening of "the moral fibre" are nowhere evident in Isabel's irresistible attraction to the old mansion, with its gloomy halls, numerous partitions, and small, shadowy rooms that "must darkle in perpetual twilight" (47). When the janitor informs her that the building has neither an elevator nor steam heat, she responds incoherently: "We'll take it, Basil, if it's like the rest" (46). He clarifies her enthusiasm, explaining: "'If it's like him, you mean.' 'I don't wonder they wanted to own them,' she hurriedly philosophized. 'If I had such a creature, nothing but death should part us, and I should no more think of giving him his *freedom*—'" (46). As Basil implies, the black janitor and the dismembered old house are closely linked in Isabel's imagination. Together they compose a figure for the "underlying nobody" that is constantly bubbling to the surface of consciousness in New York. Yet rather than retreat from this image of undifferentiated identity, Howells allows Isabel to be completely swept up in a racially charged moment of imaginative truancy. "We shall all be black in heaven—that is, black souled," she theorizes, invoking the convention of stage minstrelsy as an intriguing figure for life after death (48). Basil warns, "The next time a colored janitor opens the door to us, I'll tell him the apartment doesn't suit at the threshold. It's the only way to manage you, Isabel." "It's true," she admits, "I *am* in love with the whole race" (48). Opting for the role

Howells usually reserves for his narrator, March compliments himself for finally reining in her nonsensical enthusiasm: "If it hadn't been for my strength of character, you'd have taken an unfurnished flat without heat and with no elevator, when you had just sworn me to steam heat, an elevator, furniture, and eight hundred" (47).

The importance of this episode, which occupies two of *Hazard's* five hundred pages, should not be overemphasized. Yet as a telling exception to the rule by which Howells generally represents the authority of "character" over the free play of consciousness, the scene possesses unexpected relevance to the novel's major themes and gestures toward the central preoccupations of Howells's art. Isabel's beloved janitor is not an individual, but an ethnic type, as the narrator appears eager to emphasize when he explains that she completely fails to recognize him during a subsequent visit. Yet the janitor's status as a living, breathing nonentity, a characterless burlesque of humanity, uniquely qualifies him as a catalyst in her troubled reflections about the meaning of New York for personal identity. Whereas Beaton's egotism illustrates the moral predicament to which excessive "sophistication" inevitably leads, Isabel's janitor occupies the other end of Howells's evolutionary scale, where a coherent sense of self is equally complicated by the downward pull of an undifferentiated barbarian state. The difference between these two images of radical psychological fragmentation—of the self that "flows into everything"—is that Beaton's excesses are filtered through the narrator's moral sense, whereas the janitor's primal blackness, his perfect alignment with a cultural idea, defies moral judgement. He has not abandoned his moral foundations, like the dangerously sophisticated Beaton, for he never had any, and this lack *is* the fundamental condition of his "coon" identity. Elsewhere in the novel, as we have seen, the Marches welcome the sense of relief that comes with relaxation of the will, but their desires are tinged with serious reservations about the consequences of a too-thorough abdication of the self's authority over mental life. Here, in the caricatured black image, Howells finds it possible to celebrate the demise of "character" without "misgivings," and without resort to his customary defensive stand behind the inadequacy of language.

In his classic study of French realism, psychoanalytic critic Leo Bersani describes "the confrontation within nineteenth-century works between a structured, socially viable and verbally analyzable self and the wish to shatter psychic and social structures."[37] The realist novel, according to Bersani, tolerates psychological complexity only "as long as it doesn't threaten the ideology of the self as a fundamentally intelligent structure, unaffected by a history of fragmented, discontinuous desires" (55). The "Dean" of American letters and field marshal in the "realism war" would have resented the association, but Bersani's comments describe Howells as accurately as they describe Balzac, the gluttonous Frenchman whose fiction, in Howells's opinion, veers recklessly in the direction of caricature. Bersani notes that in his or her conflicted desire to give "coherent shape" to the "scattered or disseminated self," the realist often produces "strange, even ghoulish forms" (x). Howells's extraordinary African-American figures, whether they appear as "absolute sable" marks on the wall or as shiny manikins dressed in exaggerated finery, are the ghouls of American literary realism, the twisted signifiers of social and psychological fragmentation within the context of realism's pervasive ideology of the "intelligent self."

With characteristic insight, Howells locates Balzac's ambivalence toward a neatly organized vision of "reality" in the Frenchman's weakness for "the touch of exaggeration which typifies." Although he dismisses such lapses in Balzac's technique as vestiges of a primitive aesthetic sensibility, Howells was equally burdened with misgivings about the coherence of social and psychic structures, and—like Balzac—he betrays his ambivalence by applying "the touch of exaggeration" whenever his fiction approaches America's ethnic peripheries. Ethnic caricature, in other words, operates as a constitutive feature of Howellsian realism, which performs such awkward contortions in order to "give us," as Bersani would explain, "an image of social fragmentation contained within the order of significant form" (60).

2

"I Want a Real Coon": Twain and Ethnic Caricature

In one of Mark Twain's more fanciful variations on the theme of ethnic caricature, he imagines himself as a cholera germ injected into the blood stream of a "hoary and mouldering old bald-headed tramp" named Blitzowski, who "was shipped to America by Hungary because Hungary was tired of him."[1] In accordance with the standard periodical representation of Eastern-European immigrants, Blitzowski is "wonderfully ragged, incredibly dirty"; "he was born a thief and will die one"; "his body is a sewer, a reek of decay, a charnel house, and contains swarming nations of all the different kinds of germ-vermin that have been invented for the contentment of man" (436) (figure 2.1). As an "immigrant" among these "swarming nations," trapped on a raft within the diseased body of another immigrant, the narrator "Bkshp"—who also calls himself Huck—enjoys a unique perspective on the physical constitution of the human individual: "To my exquisite organ of vision all this spacious landscape is *alive*—alive and in energetic motion—unceasing motion—every detail of it! It is because I can see the individual molecules that compose it, and even the atoms which compose the molecules. . . . *Nothing is ever at rest.* . . . [E]verything is alive, everything is raging, whirling, whizzing, day and night" (447; emphasis in original).

In a Socratic exchange with his more experienced microbe friend Franklin, a yellow-fever germ, Bkshp slowly grasps the significance of his atomist insight into the nature of individuality, concluding that "two individuals combined, constitute a third individual—and yet each *continues* to be an individual" (453). Every perceived unity, according to this microcosmic fantasy, unravels in a multi-

WASTED ENERGY.

Nihilist Emigrant (noticing for the first time a steam explosion): "BEAUTIFUL! AH, WHY HAVE WE NOT THIS IN RUSSIA?"

FIGURE 2.I. *Life* I (February 1883): 74.

plicity of separate individualities at some more elemental level of analysis. The natural man, figured as an immigrant tramp, illiterate, "unspeakably profane," perfectly lacking in the refinements of civilization, and, like Pap Finn, covered in mud, fails as the ne plus ultra of human degeneration because "Blitzowski" is simply a name for thousands of swarming individuals who are themselves mere composites of an infinite set of atomic and subatomic particles (436). According to this fluid conception of human identity, individuality is necessarily either a performance or a sham, and the individual is either a showman or a con artist.

This discovery generates meager comic dividends in "Three Thousand Years among the Microbes," and yet Bkshp's meditation on human identity is an economical expression of the basic joke Mark Twain tells whenever he employs ethnic caricature in fiction.

The joke might be summarized as follows: what appears to be one turns out to be many. Ethnic caricature initiates this logic by creating the impression of a knowable, unitary type, in this case the type of the morally and physically degenerate immigrant vagabond. A few potent clichés are sufficient to tell us all we need to know about Blitzowski, according to the usual practice of ethnic typification, because we know him already. The punch line for Twain lies in the explosive undoing of this logic, the comic stroke that reveals Blitzowski as a complex of different entities and energies. The reified image of an Eastern-European tramp collapses with Bkshp's move to an interior point of view, a perspective that allows him to see behind the apparently unitary ethnic mask.

If this structure of joking seems almost too obvious to bear analysis, it should be just as obvious that for Twain the joke never stops here. Indeed, the comic undoing of the reified ethnic image immediately presents new opportunities for ethnic stereotyping, which in turn generate yet more opportunities for comic undoing. Thus from Bkshp's microbe point of view, Blitzowski's ethnicity comes to appear irrelevant; the tramp is no longer a foreign blot on the American landscape, for he has become, to Bkshp's awakened perception, the landscape itself. Yet reified ethnic imagery is every where *within* this landscape, whose "swarming nations" of "germ-vermin," representing "many nationalities" and speaking "many languages," reinscribe precisely the same reductive categories that Bkshp's interior point of view would seem to have enabled him to transcend. Twain implies that the national, ethnic, and cultural affiliations that characterize the microbe world will themselves come to appear ridiculous from a more elemental perspective, but such a perspective will inevitably generate its own categories of identity, which will in turn become targets of satire from some even more elemental vantage. It is an endless game of trumping overly static conceptions of identity, a game that requires the steady production of reified ethnic images at a rate identical to that of their apparent transcendence. The punch line that invites us to see beyond ethnicity and nationality as fixed categories of being only makes room for those categories to reemerge at another level of analysis, and the game of packing and unpacking ethnic signifiers goes on.

Howells understood the nature of this game, and he may have intended to incite the aging humorist's waning creative energies in 1908 by encouraging Twain to revisit *Pink Marsh,* George Ade's 1897 novel about a black shoe-shine boy in Chicago. Howells admired

Ade's sympathetic treatment of gritty urban life in the Midwest, and he enjoyed Pink's rich dialect, a version of the quaint, broken English spoken by the "resplendent darkeys in livery" who populate the dim backgrounds of Howells's own fiction.[2] As Howells would have been the first to acknowledge, however, Twain's engagement with the art of ethnic caricature was of a completely different order of magnitude, and his wild enthusiasm for the novel expresses some of that difference. His ebullient response to Howells focuses on Ade's mimetic achievement:

> [M]y admiration for the book has overflowed all limits, all frontiers. I have personally known each of the characters in the book & can testify that they are all true to the facts, & as exact as if they had been drawn to scale. . . . And for once—just this once—the illustrator is the peer of the writer. The writer flashes a character onto his page in a dozen words, you turn the leaf & there he stands, alive & breathing, with his clothes on & the African ordor [sic] oozing out of him! What a picture-gallery it is, of instantly recognizable, realizable, unassailable Authentics!
>
> Pink—oh, the shiftless, worthless, loveable black darling! Howells, he deserves to live forever.[3]

Few critics have expressed such unreserved enthusiasm for this slim volume, but Howells also relished the verisimilitude of Ade's "loveable black darling," and other writers, such as James T. Farrell, observed that Pink "exists as a real person."[4] In Twain's even more animated assessment, Pink is an old acquaintance whose physical presence is accentuated by the enigmatic African "ordor" oozing from his image.

Such overheated praise for *Pink Marsh* would deserve little comment if the novel did not strenuously insist on a different reading of its central character. In fact, Ade's opening description of the shoe-shine boy deliberately buries his individuality in an inflexible racial stereotype. Pink's outlandish costume—including a double-breasted polka-dot vest, shoes that are "two sizes too large, cracked across the top and protuberant at the heel," a "high white collar," and "a light brown hat with a high crown"—marks him as a clownish urban dandy, a latter-day version of the minstrel buffoon who takes excessive care of his shabby appearance (119).[5] Moreover, Ade gives Pink's typification a contemporary resonance by defining his appearance in terms borrowed from one of the most popular songs of the era,

Ernest Hogan's "All Coons Look Alike to Me" (1896). The narrator explains that a "song of passing popularity tells that all members of the ethiopian division 'look alike.' Pink was one of a thousand—that is, so far as mere appearance was concerned" (120).

This afterthought does little to distinguish Pink from the standard "coon" characterizations of the period. His stories of urban life revolve around such hackneyed themes as gambling, chicken-stealing, courting, and brawling with lovers and brutes. The novel begins with Pink's comic meditation on how he would spend a million dollars, a standard "coon" fantasy sequence that pokes fun at the black man's ludicrous desire to purchase the tokens of white respectability. In a late chapter, Pink describes his loss of a sweetheart, again explicitly identifying himself with the unfortunate lover in Hogan's song. "I'm like 'at boy in 'e oct'oon show," he declares, before breaking into a chorus with his eyes "dreamily half-closed":

> All a-coons looks alike to me;
> I got a new beau, you see,
> An' he's jus' as good to me
> As you, niggeh, eveh daihed to be,
> He's sutny a-good to me;
> He spen's his-a money free,
> I do n' like you a-nohow;
> All a-coons looks alike to me. (176)

John T. McCutcheon's illustrations of Pink are generally sympathetic in the context of late nineteenth-century "coon" caricature, yet they do little to particularize the abbreviated comic type (figure 2.2). Indeed, Pink's characterization in picture and text is so thoroughly aligned with the conventions of "coon" imagery that the narrator declines to record the details of his physiognomy, relying instead on the reader's familiarity with visual cues: "What need to tell of the coal-black face, the broad-flanged nose, the elastic mouth opening on teeth of pearly whiteness, and the close growth of kinky hair?" (120).

Perhaps these are the "dozen words" with which the writer "flashes a character onto his page" in Twain's enthusiastic assessment. If so, how does such a grossly generalized image produce Twain's sense of a living, breathing individual, an "instantly recognizable" acquaintance? One is tempted to accuse Twain of the worst sort of racial insensitivity by explaining that he simply mistakes the caricature of "the shiftless, worthless, loveable black darling" for the reality

FIGURE 2.2. John T. McCutcheon, from
Pink Marsh (1898; reprint, Chicago:
University of Chicago Press, 1963).

it pretends to represent. Critics have often leveled a similar charge
against the treatment of Jim in *Adventures of Huckleberry Finn,* noting that Twain allows Jim's emerging humanity to dissolve in darky
humor at irregular intervals throughout the novel.[6] In fact, Twain's
remark that Pink deserves to "live forever" contains a mild echo of
Tom Sawyer's famously cynical desire to keep Jim enslaved forever,
so that future generations of Tom's family might enjoy the fun of
pretending to set him free. Twain's adoration of Pink Marsh, like
Tom's interest in liberating Jim, might seem to depend on, rather
than to challenge, the perpetuation of a degrading comic image.

But to treat Mark Twain's relation to racial caricature as a blind
spot in his thinking about race is to dismiss one of his most compelling literary resources. From his early attendance at travelling
minstrel shows in the 1840s to his adoring remarks about Pink
Marsh in 1908, Twain was thoroughly knowledgeable about an
elaborate repertoire of conventions governing the comic representation of racial and ethnic difference. Indeed, far from betraying confusion about the nature of Pink's characterization, his letter to Howells subtly participates in the logic of "coon" comedy by dwelling on
a conventional motif, the paradox of the "real coon." This oxymoronic formulation had become standard fare in playhouses across

the country thanks to the success of entertainers such as Bert Williams and George Walker, "The Two Real Coons," who became famous for performing songs that played on the tension between an imagined authentic black identity and the burlesque conventions of traditional blackface performance.⁷

As black artists who performed "coon" songs in blackface, Walker and Williams embodied the paradox of the "real coon" with striking immediacy, but white stars were just as likely to appreciate the instability of the "coon" representation as a comic opportunity. In "I Want a Real Coon," Dolly Dorothy complains about her shiftless lover and then sings: "I want a real coon, handsome genteel coon, coon like one of my relations, I don't want no imitations."⁸ Identifying a "real coon" as one who effectively mimics genteel white standards, the song pursues a familiar racist logic by poking fun at the impossible notion of authentic black identity. In the second verse, Dolly affirms that the "real coon" of her title exists only as a fictional convention:

> Now I wants to have a real coon like the swell coons that I
>   see,
> I've seen'm at the theatre all life long,
> They will dance a round up-on the stage with clothes way
>   up in G,
> An' they take me clear to heaben with a song.
> But coons aroun' my neighborhood, they don't dress up a
>   bit,
> Oh compared to dem stage folks the rest are jays,
> So I'm willin' eb'ry time, to give up my little dime,
> Jes' to watch the real coon with his winnin' ways.

The song insists on defining the reality of the "coon" image in terms of its artificiality, a standard gesture in "coon" symbology. The point is reinforced graphically on the title page, where the caricatured image of a pompous black dandy, the "real coon" of Dorothy's song, appears juxtaposed against a photograph of the lavishly costumed white actress, whose figure bears the inscription: "The real coon singer, Dolly Dorothy" (figure 2.3). These images frame a question that the song ponders inconclusively: is the "real coon" the black man who strives pathetically to imitate white gentility or the white singer who performs her lament in blackface? In either case, "real" here denotes "imitation," much as the term "coon" simultaneously fixes and destabilizes a racial category. As a key element in the

FIGURE 2.3. Special Sheet Music
Collection, Knight Library,
University of Oregon.

comic lexicon of the 1890s, the "real coon" formulation tested the
unstable ground between authenticity and imitation, suspending
those terms in a precarious comic discourse on the nature of race
and identity.

Mark Twain participates in this discourse and pursues its logic
when he offers to "testify" on behalf of Pink Marsh, affirming that
Ade's character is "true to the facts," "alive & breathing." These expansive claims do not simply overlook the fact that Pink's identity is
conceived in terms of the maxim "all coons look alike to me"; rather,
Twain enacts the paradox of the "real coon" by attributing Pink's authenticity to conventions of graphic caricature. Pink is "as exact" as
if he had been "drawn to scale"; Ade does not write, but "flashes a
character onto his page"; the novel is a "picture-gallery" of "instantly
recognizable, realizable, unassailable Authentics." The authenticity
of the literary representation here depends upon its correspondence

to a series of visual metaphors that stress brevity of composition, boldness of outline, and instantaneous recognition. In other words, Pink is "real" to the extent that his image becomes a literary and graphic demonstration of Ernest Hogan's famous premise, which is to say that he is not "real" in the usual sense at all (figure 2.4).

This macabre joke may even account for the puzzling neologism in Twain's letter to Howells. The "African ordor oozing out" of Pink's graphically embodied image may be the result of a simple misspelling, or Twain may have intended "ordor" as a conflation of "ardor" and "odor."[9] The second explanation may be too fanciful, but the collision of these culturally loaded terms is nonetheless suggestive. As an abstract evocation of human zeal, vigor, and passionate intensity, the notion of "African ardor" might indicate Twain's interest in abandoning the standard "coon" representation; "African odor," on the other hand, revives the basest dehumanizing techniques of traditional black

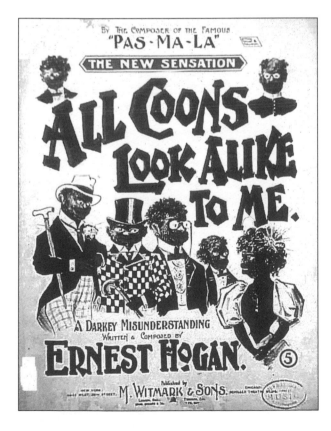

FIGURE 2.4. Special Sheet Music Collection, Knight Library, University of Oregon.

caricature. The portmanteau of these two terms, like the oxymoronic "real coon" of popular song, suspends these possibilities in an uncomfortable balance.

George Ade's admirers have generally sought to upset this balance by dismissing graphic and literary caricature as unfortunate accidents of presentation. For Farrell, the exterior trappings of "coon" identity can be overlooked, because Pink possesses "an inner core of dignity which sets him apart from the caricatures . . . of a later date."[10] A similar surface/depth model informs Larzer Ziff's opinion that Pink, "caricatured as he was, nevertheless brought to Ade's readers a stronger sense of the existence of another world, a Negro world, in their midst than they had ever had."[11] My reason for dwelling at such inordinate length on Ade's minor novel is not to challenge these sensible comments, but rather to demonstrate how differently Mark Twain constructs the relationship between the caricatured image and its object. Whereas Farrell and Ziff, anticipating the direction of much Twain criticism, labor to rescue Pink's "inner core of dignity" from the demeaning caricature through which it is presented, Twain's letter characteristically tangles the authentic Pink with his typic image at every opportunity. Whereas for Farrell, Ade's achievement lies in having "saved [Pink] from stereotype,"[12] Twain locates the shoe-shine boy's identity precisely in his conformity to a visual lexicon of racial types, "a picture gallery of . . . unassailable Authentics."

These "Authentics" are the "real coons" of song and stage, staple features of American popular culture in the racially charged 1890s. They embody a paradox that contemporary audiences willingly endured because the imaginative force of the "coon" designation so thoroughly outweighed any threat posed by the song's playfully subversive note of uncertainty. Readers today may be more eager to dismantle the paradox of the "real coon" by explaining that "coons" are not "real," yet it is a paradox that Mark Twain embraced and that his writings continually reproduced as part of an ongoing inquiry into the nature of identity. Twenty-five years before Ernest Hogan's song sparked a national craze for "coon" representations, Twain was already pushing the conceptual limits of racial and ethnic caricature in sketches such as "John Chinaman in New York," which appeared in the 1870 *Galaxy* series.[13] The narrator of the sketch appears to occupy moral high ground on the issue of racial typification by casting himself in the role of a benevolent citizen, who objects to the use of a living Chinaman as an advertisement for "one of those monster

American tea stores in New York" (231). Struck by the insult to the Chinaman's disguised humanity, the narrator delivers a sanctimonious critique of the popular practice of ethnic caricature: "Is it not a shame that we, who prate so much about civilization and humanity, are content to degrade a fellow-being to such an office as this? Is it not time for reflection when we find ourselves willing to see in such a being, matter for frivolous curiosity instead of regret and grave reflection?" (231).

Much like Pink Marsh, the Chinaman is presented through a catalogue of ethnic cues, including a "quaint Chinese hat, with peaked roof and ball on top," a "long queue dangling down his back," "blue cotton, tight-legged pants, tied close around the ankles," and "clumsy blunted shoes with thick cork soles" (232). Alone among his fellow New Yorkers, the narrator appreciates the reifying consequences of this exaggerated performance of ethnic identity, and he faults his compatriots for deriving entertainment from such a degrading spectacle. Yet the narrator's empathy for "the friendless Mongol" reproduces a version of the stereotype in the process of imagining what it obscures. The narrator wonders "what was passing behind this sad face" and then speculates: "Were his thoughts with his heart, ten thousand miles away, beyond the billowy wastes of the Pacific? among the rice-fields and the plumy palms of China? under the shadows of remembered mountain-peaks, or in groves of bloomy shrubs and strange forest-trees unknown to climes like ours?" (232).

The narrator's genteel humanism becomes the satirical target of the sketch with this demonstration of his inability to imagine anything behind the Chinaman's "sad face" except another set of exaggerated ethnic clichés. The critique of ethnic caricature becomes a kind of ethnic caricature, a polite version of the degrading imagery the narrator deplores. Moreover, the xenophobic impulse behind his apparent sympathy emerges clearly in the narrator's appeal to national values: "It is not America that treats you in this way. . . . America has a broader hospitality for the exiled and oppressed. Money shall be raised—you shall go back to China" (232).

Surely the exiled and oppressed have little use for this sort of hospitality, which urges the repatriation of ethnic types, even as it challenges the morality of comic typification. Twain pokes fun at the false assumptions underlying the narrator's self-serving humanism, but the story does not settle for such an easily gained satiric point. "What wages do they pay you?" asks the narrator, finally engaging his protégé in dialogue, to which the Chinaman responds in a thick

Irish brogue: "Divil a cint but four dollars a week and find meself; but it's aisy, barrin the troublesome furrin clothes that's so expensive" (232).

As so often in Twain's stories and sketches, an unexpectedly rich vernacular voice, charged with ethnic identifiers, explodes the false assumptions of a genteel narrator, whose formal diction connotes artificial and hypocritical values. It turns out there *is* an individual behind the crude ethnic mask, but one who fails to conform to the narrator's contrived image of "the friendless Mongol." Beneath these layers of popular and genteel stereotype lies the "real" exile, a version of Dolly Dorothy's "real coon," who ironically asserts his claim to citizenship by complaining about the expensive "furrin clothes" that constitute his disguise. Of course, this bedrock image of American identity, this "inner core" of the caricatured representation, is itself a thoroughly conventional ethnic caricature, as the illustration by True Williams in *Sketches, New and Old* makes clear (figure 2.5). The simian features that leer from beneath a "quaint Chinese hat" in Williams's engraving are a graphic reminder that every effort to pierce the mask of ethnic disguise produces only another set of cultural clichés. The layering of false identities is apparently endless, for the "real" self in Twain's sketch, as in Dolly Dorothy's song, is never safely distinguishable from its comic representation.

Of course, in affirming that every ethnic identity is "really" the

FIGURE 2.5. True Williams, from *Sketches, New and Old* (1875; reprint, New York: Oxford University Press, 1996).

caricatured performance of some other ethnic identity, the "John Chinaman" sketch underscores the threat such images pose to the narrator's *own* sense of racial prestige, a threat he all but acknowledges as he quietly retreats from the scene of his embarrassment, leaving "the exile . . . at his post" (232). The narrator retreats because when ethnic identity is expressed as a set of visual clichés, like the Chinaman's peaked hat and long queue, there is finally nothing to prevent an Irishman from becoming a Chinaman or, for that matter, an "American." In their analysis of the double-edged satirical purpose of popular cultural forms more generally, Peter Stallybrass and Allon White explain that "the very subjects which [bourgeois culture] politically excludes" become "exotic costumes which it assumes in order to play out the disorders of its own identity."[14] Here the ethnic subject's grotesque susceptibility to reification, which no degree of sentimental humanism can undo, provokes a rethinking of the narrator's own claims to a privileged social status based on the presumed integrity of ethnic classifications.

Stallybrass and White are careful to note that this reflexive feature of bourgeois entertainments, whereby the dominant culture speaks "to itself in the delirium of its repressed others," does not produce a "necessary or automatic political progressiveness."[15] Indeed, even to speculate about the political progressiveness of late nineteenth-century racial and ethnic caricatures is to obscure the profound nativist anxiety that fueled such images and supported their popularity. It must be acknowledged that caricatures of ethnic subjects typically have the unambiguous function of exaggerating physical and cultural characteristics in order to make ethnic identity an inflexible and irresistible condition of being. No matter how desperately E. W. Kemble's "coons" work to mimic respectable white behavior and appearance, Kemble's humor hinges on their violent failure to become anything except what they are and must remain. Ben Jerome conveys the same reassuring thought in "Nothin' But a Coon," a popular rag whose unambiguous title articulates the song's central premise that efforts at ethnic disguise actually confirm the unalterable condition of ethnic identity.[16]

Yet if the caricatured image exaggerates racial and ethnic differences in order to shore up the fire walls of "American" identity, guaranteeing that an Irishman will always be an Irishman and that "all coons look alike," the same images work to destabilize the very categories they are meant to police. As the *Galaxy* sketch begins to suggest, Twain's complicated engagement with late nineteenth-century ethnic caricature and its antebellum precursor, blackface minstrelsy, hinges on the rich uncertainty generated by modes of representation that perform the dual functions of propping up and laughing down an excessively static conception of identity. At the level of style and sensibility, Twain may have shared little in common with other writers grouped awkwardly under the conceptual umbrella of "American literary realism," but commitment to this double purpose in an era of increasingly rigid ethnic classification stands out as a unique point of agreement among writers for whom the power of the exaggerated ethnic image lay in its ability to accommodate radically dissimilar cultural meanings.[17]

Dolly Dorothy conveys some of this double purpose by juxtaposing notions of authentic and imitation selfhood in her image of the "real coon," a phrase whose economy and ambiguity Twain almost matches with his infamous characterization of "the genuine nigger show."[18] This book cannot pretend to offer new information about the historical practice of blackface minstrelsy, which in recent years has received generous attention from cultural historians, musicologists, literary scholars, and others.[19] Nevertheless, it is essential to locate Twain's engagement with the conventions of ethnic and racial caricature within the context of his thinking about the disappearing art of minstrel performance. Writing in 1906, at the height of the "coon" era, he mourned the death of traditional racial burlesque and the emergence of the degenerate variety show: "Birch, Wambold, and Backus are gone years ago, and with them departed to return no more forever, I suppose, the real nigger show—the genuine nigger show, the extravagant nigger show" (110). As a stage convention, he explains, minstrelsy "was born in the early forties and it had a prosperous career for about thirty-five years; then it degenerated into a variety show and was nearly all variety show with a negro act or two thrown in incidentally" (114–15). Howells provides a glimpse of this degenerate form when a character in *Letters Home* catalogues the bill of fare at a turn-of-the-century variety show in New York: "[T]he girl with the Southern accent that sings pathetic ballads of the lost cause, and then coon songs for her recalls; . . . the tremendously fashionable comedy sketch, all butlers and footmen . . .; the Viennese dancers, and the German acrobats and acrobatesses; the colored monologuist . . .; they were all there and more too."[20]

To Mark Twain's dismay, the variety show's frantic combination of physical stunts, melodrama, and ethnic mimicry emerged at the close of the nineteenth century to replace the minstrel show's more concentrated and consistent racial burlesque. But Twain's nostalgia for the "genuine nigger show" involved a more complex sense of degradation than this development alone can account for. As his musings on the dynamics of early minstrel performance make clear, the object of his nostalgia was an attitude toward racial mimicry, an attitude capable of accommodating what Eric Lott calls minstrelsy's "oscillation between currency and counterfeit."[21] The endmen, "Bones" and "Banjo," according to Twain's reminiscence, appeared on stage "with coal-black hands and faces and their clothing was a loud and extravagant burlesque of the clothing worn by the plantation slave of the time" (111). There is no question that this loud burlesque functioned to demean its African-American subject, exposing the black male to ridicule through a distorted representation, but in a characteristic afterthought Twain insists that the extravagance of the minstrel's costume also connoted a radical authenticity: "not that the rags of the poor slave were burlesqued, for that would not have been possible; burlesque could have added nothing in the way of extravagance to the sorrowful accumulations of rags and patches which constituted his costume" (111). When reality is so extravagant that burlesque can do nothing to exaggerate its conditions, racial caricature becomes a kind of realism. Once again, I do not mean to imply that Twain merely confuses the minstrel representation for the reality it pretends to represent. Rather, as with his adoring comments about the "authentic" Pink Marsh, Twain relishes ethnic burlesque for its power to set in motion an uncertain relationship between reality and representation, the "genuine" subject and its "extravagant" embodiment. Authenticity and imitation, Lott's "currency and counterfeit," become two sides of the same coin when reality itself is conceived as a burlesque performance of ethnic identity.

Poised between the plantation types Bones and Banjo, the middleman also performed a vital function in Twain's conception of the minstrel show. According to his 1906 account, "Mr. Johnson" wore elegant attire and addressed his fellow minstrels in a haughty imitation of proper English: "He was clothed in the faultless evening costume of the white society gentleman and used a stilted, courtly, artificial, and painfully grammatical form of speech, which the innocent villagers took for the real thing as exhibited in high and citified society, and they vastly admired it and envied the man who could frame it on the spot without reflection and deliver it in this easy and fluent and artistic fashion" (111–12).

As this account suggests, Mr. Johnson's part in the minstrel show involved a two-way burlesque, which produced a rich sense of confusion about who was imitating whom. In contrast to the grotesque sensuality of Bones and Banjo, whose "sorrowful accumulation of rags and patches" owed nothing to burlesque, the role of the middleman belonged to a white man imitating a black man imitating a white man, and doing so with such facility that "the innocent villagers" accepted his performance as "the real thing." Without this confusion over "the real thing" and its relation to the caricatured image, minstrelsy degenerates into the mere variety show, according to Twain's analysis, and—just as important—members of the minstrel audience, instead of participating in complex acts of identification and repudiation, settle into comfortable, passive spectatorship.

More than any single change in the formal aspect of blackface performance, this transition from active engagement with minstrelsy's unstable representations to self-assured spectatorship brought an end to Twain's "genuine nigger show," as the cultural historians Lawrence Levine, David Roediger, and Dale Cockrell have explained.[22] Roediger demonstrates that early blackface extravaganzas occasionally triggered racial violence in northern cities, and Cockrell confirms that even within the formalized space of the antebellum theater minstrelsy was "startling in its immediacy."[23] Tracing blackface performance to its beginnings in British and European folk theatricals, including mumming plays and callithumpian revelries, Cockrell explains that minstrelsy originated in a domestic setting, in the kitchen or living room, where a marauding troop of entertainers performed inversive satire for an audience expected to comment freely on the quality of the performance (58–59). In making its way to the American stage in the late 1820s, blackface inevitably sacrificed some of its intimacy, but reports of audience behavior confirm that early nineteenth-century theatergoers considered spontaneous response an essential component of the show (16–17). The word "minstrelsy" was first attached to blackface in the 1840s as part of an effort to associate such low-brow entertainment with the more legitimate conventions of the musical concert, and this calculated misrepresentation invited a further withdrawal of the audience, which was now expected to listen (151).[24] Cockrell explains that by the 1840s managers were making the theater "darker, quieter, more secure, and more private" in a deliberate attempt to remove audiences "from the visceral and essentially performative" aspect of early racial burlesque (60). In order to guarantee the transformation of blackface performance into a legitimate form of musical theater, managers "enforced a new code of behavior, one that led to the theater becoming . . . a private space for reflection, in effect a temple of culture whose sacralization was complete by late century" (149).[25]

With the emergence of a more private, passive, and respectable audience, minstrelsy's communal significance underwent a corresponding change. Among the callithumpian rituals that gave birth to blackface performance, perhaps the most intriguing was the *charivari*, or shivaree, as it was sometimes called in America. Cockrell describes the *charivari* as a "ritual of communal regulation," in which young males, masked in chimney soot and grease, terrorized individuals "adjudged to be undermining the social cohesion of the community" (33). Visiting the offender at night, the blackface intruders would engage in "short term destruction of the domestic peace to ensure long-term communal security" (33). The practice of tarring and feathering is a relatively modern variant of the *charivari*, which developed numerous forms of expression according to historical and cultural circumstances, in each case functioning to enforce compliance with communal norms. Early stage minstrelsy, with its potent satire of Jacksonian political culture and withering parody of social pretension, black and white, preserved some of this disruptive communal function, allowing the audience to laugh together at outlandish representations of social deviance. Moreover, the *charivari* remained closely linked to the emergence of graphic caricature throughout the nineteenth century, lending its name to Philipon's journal, arguably Europe's most important humor periodical until the founding of *Punch,* which identified itself as "*the London 'Charivari'* " (figure 2.6). This ubiquitous word is associated with the German *Kladderdatsch,* a Teutonic spin-off of the highly successful French and British magazines, and even America's *Puck,* with its orthographic allusion to London's *Punch,* can claim to be descended from the greased and sooty marauders of the original *charivari.*

For all the apparent continuity of this pedigree, the communal dimension of the nineteenth-century minstrel show and its graphic offspring gradually waned in response to changes in the performative context of blackface entertainment, as Twain observes in a telling anecdote.[26] Many years after the minstrel show had begun its downward slide, he remembers having escorted his mother and Aunt Betsey Smith to a performance by the Christy Minstrels in St. Louis. As proper churchgoers, according to Twain's story, the elderly women had never attended such an event, and he persuades them to

FIGURE 2.6. Legend for Philipon's *Le Charivari.*

accompany him only by claiming that the evening's entertainment
will consist of "an exhibition of native African music by fourteen
missionaries . . . just returned from the dark continent" (116).
Comforted by the righteousness of their expectations, the two
women enter the great hall of the Mercantile Library with sixteen
hundred more seasoned theater-goers, and "[w]hen the grotesque
negroes came filing out on the stage in their extravagant costumes,
the old ladies were almost speechless with astonishment. I explained
to them that the missionaries always dressed like that in Africa"
(116). When Aunt Betsey objects, "But they're niggers," her escort
responds resourcefully: "That is no matter; they are Americans in a
sense, for they are employed by the American Missionary Society"
(117).

Rather than appease the naive outrage of his companions by in-
forming them that the performers are really white—a fact that escapes no one else in the audience—Twain redoubles the minstrel
show's tired masquerade. He augments rather than dissipates his
mother's confusion by grounding the authenticity of the performance in a new layer of ethnic disguise, in effect restoring minstrelsy's
atrophied dialectic in the process of describing it. Moreover, Twain's
repackaging of the Christy performers has a crucial effect on the
show's function as *charivari.* When the actors deliver a threadbare
joke that members of the audience have heard hundreds of times before, "a frozen and solemn and indignant silence" settles upon the
house, until, the punch line delivered, the old ladies "threw their
heads back and went off into heart-whole cackles and convulsions of

laughter that so astonished and delighted that great audience that it rose in a solid body to look and see who it might be that had not heard that joke before" (117–18). Their infectious laughter fills the hall, until "the whole sixteen hundred joined in and shook the place with the thunders of their joy" (118).

Clearly this is less an account of minstrelsy in the final hours of its waning popularity than a fantasy of social renewal, a momentary reversal in the emergence of a new theater audience at the end of the nineteenth century. In reassuring his mother and Aunt Betsey that the performance amounts to a genuine representation of cultural practices, "an exhibition and illustration of native African music," Twain restores a collective appreciation for the dynamic uncertainty that once animated "the genuine nigger show." By the latter part of the nineteenth century, according to this complicated historical account, blackface performance was no longer "genuine" in the sense that its bogus claims to authenticity no longer animated the response of a community, which here rises "in a solid body" perhaps for the last time. As Pierre Bourdieu might explain, the working class engagement characteristic of early minstrel audiences has been displaced by self-assured bourgeois spectatorship, a distinction further reinforced by Twain's observation to his mother "that the best people in St. Louis were present, and that certainly they would not be present if the show were not of a proper sort" (117).[27] These "jaded souls," as Twain calls them, can experience the inversive energies of racial burlesque only through vicarious participation in the naive confusion of Mrs. Clemens and Aunt Betsey, confusion inspired by Twain's deliberate fudging of the line between high and low entertainment, authentic cultural display and mere racial caricature (118). The "genuine nigger show," as that offensive term is calculated to imply, constituted such a line in the very act of breaching it. The degeneration of minstrelsy as a public spectacle represented for Twain a dismantling of the oxymoronic logic of the "genuine nigger show" by an audience impatient with racial and ethnic ambiguity.

This was the audience Mark Twain shared with *Puck, Judge, Century,* and *Harper's Monthly.* During the last twenty years of the nineteenth century, ethnic images migrated from the declining minstrel stage to the pages of America's burgeoning magazine industry, where a new generation of caricaturists fashioned forms of racial and ethnic burlesque to suit the demands of a new medium and a new audience. Late nineteenth-century ethnic caricature may be nothing more than the graphic residue of minstrelsy's complex blend of "loathing and desire," a less nuanced expression of white middle-class ambivalence over "the scarifying vision of human regression," but Twain was keenly attentive to changes that produced the more virulently racist iconology of the post-Reconstruction era.[28] As minstrelsy's public spectacle yielded to the more private experience of ethnic caricature in novels and magazines, the images themselves developed in response to a new set of anxieties, including unprecedented fears about immigration, miscegenation, and "race suicide."[29] Whereas minstrel caricature hinged on doubleness, clouding the distinction between authentic and imitation selfhood in a dynamic and often erotic ambiguity, graphic caricatures of the late nineteenth century tended to forestall identification with the caricatured subject, offering the embattled bourgeois self a measure of false confidence by projecting racial identity as a foundational category of being.

No single image can document this shift in racial feeling, but a 1901 illustration in *Puck* marks the distance separating minstrelsy's ambiguous racial transgressions from the very different sensibility of late nineteenth-century "coon" caricature (figure 2.7). In the *Puck* illustration, three black children stand outside a stage door where a dramatic version of *Uncle Tom's Cabin* is playing. A girl, apparently dressed for the theater in her best imitation of bourgeois finery, stares at a billboard image of Topsy—clothed in rags, grinning from ear to ear—and asks her companion, "Mean ter say she's a white gal?" The comedy here lies in the juxtaposition of two exaggerated ethnic performances, as both girls attempt to breach the color line with the paraphernalia of racial disguise. Minstrelsy's "oscillation between currency and counterfeit" might seem to be fully at play in the boy's coy response, "In course she is," a malapropism that neatly emphasizes the white actress's capacity for racial metamorphosis. Yet in keeping with the mood and sentiment of late nineteenth-century caricature, the illustration raises the specter of fluid racial transgression only to neutralize its threat. "Golly!," concludes the girl, "I reckon no cullud gal cud look as much like a white gal as dat gal looks like a cullud gal." With this expression of "admiration," the black subject affirms that minstrelsy's inversive energies move in only one direction. For all its play with notions of authenticity and imitation, inspired by apparently symmetrical acts of racial imposture, the sketch finally deploys blackface to insist that no disguise can turn a black girl into a white girl.

This assertion conveys the essence of "coon" comedy, which

ADMIRATION.

"Mean ter say she's a white gal?"
"In course she is."
"Golly! I reckon no cullud gal cud look as much like a
white gal as dat gal looks like a cullud gal."

FIGURE 2.7. *Puck* 49 (April 1901).

Twain recognized as a significant departure from the transgressive
antics of antebellum minstrelsy. Whether or not we accept his romantic account of the "pristine purity" of the old time minstrel
show, it is important to understand his use of ethnic burlesque in the
context this transition to a new vocabulary of ethnic images.[50] The
complexity of his relation to those images, however, cannot be overstated, for although Twain lamented the decline of minstrel comedy
and the emergence of a modern audience made up of "jaded souls,"
he was unquestionably one of the chief purveyors of "coon" comedy
at the end of the nineteenth century. *Adventures of Huckleberry Finn*
made Kemble famous for his depiction of "the black type," as Kemble explained in a retrospective essay, and the novel may therefore be
credited with having inaugurated a vogue for "coon" caricatures that
lasted well into the twentieth century.[31] When Twain needed an illustrator for *Huckleberry Finn*, he did not consult with trained artists
but made an informal search through "the comic papers," including
Puck, Judge, and *Life*, which by 1884 were already notorious for spe-
cializing in distorted ethnic representations.[32] In an insightful essay,
Earl Briden demonstrates that Kemble had established his reputa-

FIGURE 2.8. E. W. Kemble, from
Adventures of Huckleberry Finn
(1885; reprint, Berkeley:
University of California Press, 1985).

tion as a caricaturist of black life before receiving the *Huckleberry Finn* commission, which probably reflected Twain's appreciation for Kemble's "coon" images in *Life* and *The Daily Graphic*.[33] One *Life* image in particular bears a striking resemblance to Kemble's conception of Jim in *Huckleberry Finn*, implying that Twain's choice of Kemble represented a conscious effort to insert his narrative of antebellum life into the rapidly emerging post-Reconstruction graphic discourse on racial and ethnic identity (figures 2.8 and 2.9).[34]

FIGURE 2.9. *Life* 2
(September 1883): 113.

Briden's conclusions are damning: Jim is "a comic type border-
ing on caricature, his features and postures exaggerated, with the result that any distinct personality and individual reality are absorbed
into what amounts to a racial abstraction." For all the novel's gestures at liberation, its black hero remains—at the textual and pictorial levels—"fast in the grip of comic typification."[35] Other scholars
have reached similar conclusions. For Guy Cardwell, Twain's representation of Jim as a comic type is evidence of the author's enduring
racism, despite genteel affectations he developed in the refined atmosphere of Hartford.[36] Ellen Moers captures the flavor of Twain's
collaboration with Kemble when she comments that "stupidity,
shiftlessness, superstition, helpless immaturity, and ineradicable ignorance are the qualities we find in Twain's Negroes."[37] Reading
Kemble's illustrations in relation to *Huckleberry Finn*, Douglass Anderson concurs that some images of Jim "are so heavily dependent
on the appetite for racial stereotypes in Twain's audience that they
constitute a virtual case study in the visual expression of racial
pathology."[38] Perhaps the most forceful statement of this popular
view has been advanced by Fredrick Woodard and Donnarae Mac-
Cann, who argue that "Twain's use of the minstrel tradition under-
cuts serious consideration of Jim's humanity beyond those qualities
stereotypically attributed to the noble savage; and Jim is forever
frozen within the convention of the minstrel darky."[39]

More sympathetic critics have been quick to excuse Twain for
the novel's vexed relation to a long tradition of ethnic stereotyping.
Howells was among the first to insist that Twain's representation of
African Americans contained "not an ungenerous line,"[40] and a
modern equivalent of this opinion has been strenuously argued by
Shelley Fisher Fishkin, whose work has focused critical attention on
Huckleberry Finn's deep investments in black culture, belying the
image of Twain as a mere caricaturist of black life.[41] Other critics
have questioned Twain's attitude toward Kemble's illustrations, suggesting that the author only reluctantly agreed to include Kemble's
"coon" images as graphic companions to an otherwise antiracist narrative.[42] According to this view, illustrations of Jim as a slack-jawed
fool, such as in figure 2.8, fail to appreciate his subtle management
of the slave regime. Ralph Ellison, David Smith, and other sensitive
readers have advanced this generous interpretation by explaining
that the textual Jim is a skillful trickster who profits from his ability
to play a role, even if Kemble's crude drawings convey no hint of his
depth.[43]

Whether they absolve Twain of responsibility for the novel's reliance on racial caricatures or condemn him for the same features of
the text, these comments all treat the exaggerated ethnic image as a
regrettable mistake, a default on the novel's unsure commitment to
the humanitarian impulse of literary realism, which might be boiled
down to Howells's statement that "men are more alike than unalike
one another."[44] But Twain's commitment to this impulse, as we have
seen in numerous examples already, was no more stable than his
commitment to the idea that "all coons look alike," or that "a coon
ain't nothin' but a coon." As the labored satire of "Three Thousand
Years among the Microbes" suggests, these assertions of static ethnic
identity operate in Twain's fiction as set-up lines for the comic stroke
that explodes the illusion of unitary identity, affirming for the moment (at least until the inevitable next set-up line) that "men are
more alike than unalike." The difference between Howells and
Twain on the issue of ethnic caricature is that Howells really believes
in this statement, such that his exaggerated ethnic figures serve as a
way of importing into his fiction what Howells treats as an almost illicit ambiguity over the nature of "character." Twain, on the other
hand, is far more invested in the game of ethnic misrepresentation
than in any one of its possible outcomes. Jim is a "coon" at moments
in the novel so that we may take pleasure in the undoing of that fiction, and he is almost immediately a "coon" again so that we may
again enjoy, with Tom Sawyer, the wholesome "fun" of setting him
conceptually free. Twain understands that these two movements—
one that imposes ridiculous conceptual limitations on the individual, one that dismantles those limitations with self-congratula-
tory élan—produce two different kinds of pleasure in his audience,
and he is willing to take his laughs wherever he can get them. Ultimately, however, these two movements are part of a single process,
the same process that sustained the popularity of Walker and
Williams, "The Two Real Coons," and that informed Twain's complex nostalgia for "the genuine nigger show." To rescue Jim from the
indignities imposed on him throughout the novel, either by condemning the author or by explaining that Jim is not really demeaned
when Twain dresses him in blackface, is to bring this process to an
end. We may decide that this is a necessary response to a work of fiction that often borders on outright racism, but in this case we should
not imagine that we are encountering the full force of Mark Twain's
humor.

To allow ourselves this encounter is to assume an extremely

questionable relation to a novel that has a great deal to say about the way audiences do and do not act. According to the account of his mother's evening at the St. Louis Mercantile Library, minstrelsy's unpredictable, inversive humor collapses when racial burlesque fails to surprise its audience into collective expressions of identification and disgust. Without a convincing set-up, the punch line simply lands flat. Like the autobiographical anecdote, which ends in riotous communal laughter, *Adventures of Huckleberry Finn* seeks both to chronicle and to repair this loss of dynamic interaction. The novel repeatedly laments the emergence of disengaged spectatorship as a model of audience behavior *within* Huck's antebellum world, even as it offers frequent minstrel interludes as a strategy for recuperating the inversive energy of early blackface performance among the novel's readers.[45]

The murder of Boggs, one of many episodes from which Jim is conspicuously absent, demonstrates the way audiences typically behave within the novel.[46] Boggs meets his fate in Bricksville, a town defined by its passive enjoyment of violent entertainment. The loafers who line the main street are in a constant state of repose until a dog attacks a sow, "and then you would see all the loafers get up and watch the thing out of sight, and laugh at the fun and look grateful for the noise. Then they'd settle back again till there was a dog fight" (183). Boggs's "little old monthly drunk" is a regular feature of this routine (183). After twenty years of repetition, his tall-talking performance has lost its power to engage his audience, but he is tolerated and even appreciated as another welcome distraction from the town's collective lethargy. One member of the audience, however, rejects this bankrupt interaction between hackneyed performance and passive response. "I'm tired of this," exclaims Colonel Sherburn, expressing neither outrage nor anger but a more profound sense of despair over the decay of performative rituals that have lost their hold on the imagination (184).

The death of Boggs might seem to represent a violent disruption of the town's passive consumption of degenerate entertainment, but in fact his murder only produces a new script for an old and familiar drama, one fully in keeping with the town's regular diversions. Their voyeuristic interest piqued rather than dispelled, the loafers push and shove outside the drugstore window, vying with Huck for a glimpse of the dying man. A mob quickly forms in active response not to the murder but to its amateur reenactment by a "lanky man, with long hair and a big white fur stove-pipe hat on the back of his head" (187). The murder, which intends to put an end to atrophied performance, becomes one more performance in Bricksville's endless repertoire, each one more violent than the last, each one more symptomatic of a culture in decline. The storm of enthusiasm that fuels the mob's demand for a public lynching, an aberration of the traditional *charivari,* is a mockery of collective audience response, as Sherburn confirms when he disperses the crowd with his blistering cynicism.

In pointed contrast to Bricksville and the corrupt cultural life of the shore stands the fragile pastoral dimension of Twain's Mississippi Valley, also a world defined by the quality of its performances. This is the world of Huck and Jim alone on the raft or hiding out in the woods, talking about Solomon, Frenchmen, royalty, books, and finance. As Anthony Berret has demonstrated, these comic exchanges reproduce the minstrel stage even as the novel chronicles its displacement by degenerate forms of entertainment. According to Berret, the novel mirrors the minstrel show's three-part structure, including an opening sequence of comic dialogues, an "olio" featuring novelty acts like those of the king and duke, and "an elaborate, zany burlesque."[47] The novel's reliance on standard blackface material and minstrel techniques, including especially Twain's use of a black vernacular mouthpiece for his blend of social criticism and high pathos, also suggests that *Huckleberry Finn* can be read as a kind of literary minstrel show. But to embrace this view too closely is to overlook the novel's persistent critique of social pathologies unique to the "coon" era. As Twain clearly understood when he wrote of the death of minstrelsy as a symptom of cultural decline, the iconography of racial caricature took on radically new meanings at the end of the nineteenth century, meanings that in some cases—*Puck*'s "Admiration" is a representative example—explicitly cancel the inversive force of early minstrel performance. *Huckleberry Finn* participates in this transformation, setting a new standard for "coon" imagery in fiction and illustration, even as Twain strains to resurrect the defunct comedy of early racial burlesque.

If the novel succeeds in recuperating minstrelsy's atrophied dialectic, it does so significantly only in the imaginary space that separates Huck and Jim from any potential audience. In one famously controversial episode—which Twain himself performed on stage, enacting his own problematic version of a late nineteenth-century minstrel show—Jim in the role of the endman responds to Huck's straight-faced provocations by explaining that someday he is going to be rich, and then he pauses: "I'se rich now, come to look at it. I owns mysef, en I's wuth eight hund'd dollars. I wisht I had de money, I wouldn' want no mo'" (57).[48] Jim's notion that he is at once a commodity worth eight hundred dollars and a man capable of owning that commodity is a logical absurdity, but like Twain's oxymoronic "genuine nigger show" it is a logical absurdity that bristles with ambiguous meaning. Jim's formulation conflates a bourgeois conception of possessive individualism with the reductive materialism of a slave regime that defines human value in monetary terms. Many readers are uncomfortable, as they should be, with this sort of humor, which hinges on Jim's apparently bewildered acceptance of a demeaning characterization; other readers respond defensively by maintaining that Jim is in control of the irony implied by his statement. But this is an interpretive choice we should resist. Jim's simultaneous assertion and devaluation of self-worth are for Twain the essence of minstrelsy's power, which depends on the taut ambiguity of Jim's double vision. How does one distinguish the real individual from its commodified imitation? Where is the line between the "authentic" self and its representation on stage or in fiction? Twain's "genuine nigger show" begged these questions relentlessly, inviting audiences to identify with the anxious predicament of the minstrel performer, even as the blackface mask transformed such potentially threatening identification into racist fun.[49]

Protected from the corrosive influence of an audience, Huck and Jim engage in such dubious fun, allowing minstrelsy's racial comedy to guide their discussions about fiction, history, identity, and representation. In each case, Jim's stubborn ignorance energizes the debate, much as the naïveté of Jane Clemens energizes the performance of the Christy Minstrels by confounding distinctions between "currency and counterfeit," authenticity and imitation. Beyond the limits of Twain's pastoral stage world, however, racial caricature takes on meanings more appropriate to the novel's 1885 social context. When Jim complains that lying around tied to the raft all day is "mighty heavy and tiresome," the duke dresses him as King Leer, "and then he took his theater-paint and painted Jim's face and hands and ears and neck all over a dead dull blue, like a man that's been drowned nine days. Blamed if he warn't the horriblest looking outrage I ever see" (203) (figure 2.10). If we recall Huck's conviction that Jim is "white inside," then this performance of ethnic identity represents a doubling of minstrelsy's rudimentary disguise (341). But Jim's impersonation of a "sick Arab" has more in common with late

FIGURE 2.10. E. W. Kemble, from
Adventures of Huckleberry Finn.

HARMLESS.

nineteenth-century ethnic caricature than with the minstrel show's ambiguous racial inversions, as Huck suggests in a parting comment: "he didn't only look like he was dead, he looked considerable more than that" (203, 204). Instead of complicating notions of self and authenticity, the extravagance of Jim's racial disguise merely conceals— one could say absorbs—the identity of the caricatured subject. At this point, *Huckleberry Finn* becomes a study in "coon" caricature, and its echoes of minstrel performance fade into an irretrievable pastoral background.

This is not to say that the novel develops a consistent account of the displacement of minstrel humor by "coon" caricature. In fact, Twain achieves some of his most poignant irony by inverting the racial content of standard "coon" symbolism, as when Huck appears as a chicken thief in chapter twelve. For late nineteenth-century readers, a criminal appetite for chicken amounted to shorthand notation for black identity, just as surely as the ubiquitous razor and deck of cards denoted "coon" masculinity in the era of Jim Crow (figure 2.11). Charles W. Chesnutt toyed with this powerful cultural symbol in "A Victim of Heredity; or Why the Darky Loves Chicken," and countless songs and illustrations of the period defined black difference in terms

FIGURE 2.11. E. W. Kemble, from
Adventures of Huckleberry Finn.

of this symbolic appetite (figure 2.12).[50] When Huck and Jim discuss
the morality of "borrowing" chickens, watermelons, mushmelons, "or
things of that kind," Jim articulates an ethic of moderation and
restraint, confounding the "coon" stereotype, much as Huck later
inverts the novel's racial geometry by declaring, "I'm a nigger" (79–
80, 210).

FIGURE 2.12. *Judge* 25
(September 1893): 208.

Twain enjoyed such charged moments of ethnic inversion, which recall the sudden revelation of John Chinaman's Irish origin, and yet he drew equally on the power of ethnic caricatures to fix identity according to an abstract principle. The novel returns to this pattern of joking when Tom Sawyer discovers the scene of Jim's confinement on the Phelps plantation by observing the route taken by a slice of watermelon. Enacting the lockstep rationale of "coon" comedy as a detective strategy, Tom declares, "Watermelon shows man, lock shows prisoner; and it ain't likely there's two prisoners on such a little plantation, and where the people's all so kind and good" (291) (figure 2.13). The inevitability of this logic, which defines Jim in terms of another symbolic appetite, compels Huck's admiration and Twain's sarcasm: "If I had Tom Sawyer's head, I wouldn't trade it off to be a duke, nor mate of a steamboat, nor clown in a circus, nor nothing I can think of" (291–92).

FIGURE 2.13. E. W. Kemble, from *Adventures of Huckleberry Finn.*

VITTLES.

In associating Tom's logic with the overt racism of the duke and the cheap comedy of the country circus—a prototype of the variety show—Twain makes his opinion known, but the novel seems unable to resist the degenerate entertainment he deplores. I do not mean to accuse Twain of mere opportunism or to suggest that the novel defaults on its humanitarian promise when it lapses into an offensive brand of "darky" humor. Rather, I am arguing that the drift toward an inflexible comic discourse, a movement many readers would like to denounce or to excuse, constitutes the heart of Twain's social critique of nineteenth-century America, a culture—and, for Twain, an audience—in irreversible decline. Jim's representation as a comic type in *Huckleberry Finn* draws simultaneously on an idealized minstrel dynamic and an emerging logic of "coon" caricature to narrate this decline. The novel's minstrel sequences, like Jane Clemens's evening with the Christy performers, intend to recover through memory and fantasy some of the dialectical force of early blackface performance within the context of its transformation into a new form of public entertainment. It is a strategy designed to fail, of course, given that the very images with which Twain evokes minstrelsy's defunct humor, including Kemble's caricatures, have become for the author himself potent indicators of cultural change. As he clearly understood when he wrote of the decay of public spectacles like the minstrel show, the caricatured ethnic image, although formally unchanged, had begun to serve different purposes in the late nineteenth-century. This is why Huck and Jim can perform their special brand of minstrel comedy only in moments of perfect seclusion—literally in hiding—and it is also why ethnic caricature in *Huckleberry Finn* is finally less a means of recovering the past than one more symptom of persistent cultural decline.

Twain never entirely gave up on ethnic caricature as a means of posing fundamental questions about identity. Is a man, "at bottom," a man, as Hank Morgan speculates in *A Connecticut Yankee,* or is the human individual a mere disguise for an infinite number of independent organisms, which course through the bloodstream like immigrant hordes, perpetually reconstituting a phantom land mass known as Blitzowski or America?[51] Twain's conception of the "genuine nigger show," a paradoxical blend of authenticity and imitation, animated these questions in his own imagination long after the historical decline of minstrel performance, suspending writerly commitments to realism and burlesque in a precariously entertaining balance. For all the power of burnt cork to interrogate conceptions of American identity, however, he aptly perceived that minstrelsy's graphic legacy worked to foreclose the very questions on which his humor most depended. This may be why the final efforts of Mark Twain's literary career so often resort to fantasy as a means of recreating the conditions necessary to his imagination.

3
A Jamesian Art to Be Cultivated

The problem with New York's "swarming" ethnic populations, for Henry James, was that foreigners could not be counted on to remain foreign enough.[1] "The claim of the alien," he worries in *The American Scene,* "however immeasurably alien, to share in one's supreme relation was everywhere the fixed element, the reminder not to be dodged" (85). One's "supreme relation" is "one's relation to one's country," a covenant of citizenship that is lamentably available to whatever "foreign matter" happens to wash up on the shores of Ellis Island (85, 64). James occasionally resorts to the rhetoric of the melting pot to rationalize his anxieties about his fellow New Yorkers, whom he encounters "in the first grossness of their alienism" (120). "The material of which they consist," he comforts himself, "is being dressed and prepared, at this stage, for brotherhood" (120). Time and generational change will vindicate "the ceaseless process of the recruiting of our race, of the plenishing of our huge national *pot au feu*" (64). More often, however, New York's immigrant faces produce a debilitating nativist anxiety in the restless analyst, whose search for the "treasures of type" is dogged by "a haunting wonder as to what might be becoming of us all, 'typically,' ethnically, and thereby physiognomically, linguistically, *personally*" (5, 64).

The final note in this catalogue of fears underscores the personal dimension of James's xenophobia, his persistent worry that the presence of the alien might affect the most private aspects of consciousness. Returning from Ellis Island, he speculates that the effect of such a visit "on the spirit of any sensitive citizen who may have happened to 'look in' is that he comes back . . . not at all the same person that he went" (85). It is not "the combination of their quantity and their quality" that threatens to overwhelm the analyst's sense of himself; rather, it is the alien's incongruous "note of settled possession," his air of being "at home," "so that *un*settled possession is what we, on our side, seem reduced to" (86, 125). James's anxieties about the changing physiognomy of New York—and about consequent changes to his own identity as an American—stem from this recurring insight into the unity of sensations, "the general queer sauce of New York," which covers everything with the same flavor (117). Although "the grossness of alienism" is everywhere apparent, the real threat to detached subjectivity lies in the observation that New York's immigrants are neither gross nor alien enough.

To establish a measure of critical distance from the depressing homogeneity of impressions, James adopts an aesthetic strategy already well known to readers of New York's thriving illustrated magazines. Like the ethnic caricaturists whose work regularly spiced the pages of *Harper's Monthly, Century,* and *Scribner's* throughout the late nineteenth century, James proposes to get "away from one's subject by plunging into it, for sweet truth's sake, still deeper" (126). As Thomas Nast, Frederick Opper, E. W. Kemble, and the other giants of American graphic caricature might have agreed, the way to check the encroachment of the alien upon one's sense of self, country, and culture is to *describe* him, "for sweet truth's sake." Thus James appears to have borrowed a page from the intensely anti-Semitic *Life* magazine when he responds to the "swarming," "crowded, hustled" Lower East Side by imagining that he stands "at the bottom of some vast sallow aquarium in which innumerable fish, of over-developed proboscis, were to bump together, forever, amid the heaped spoils of the sea" (131).

This striking image establishes an imaginary glass boundary between the aquatic Jews of lower Manhattan and the analyst who stands ostensibly in their midst. Throughout his tour of the city, James repeats the same paradoxical gesture, seeking out crowded spaces only to deploy exaggerated ethnic imagery as an assertion of his radical separation from the scene. Anticipating the expert curatorship of Adam Verver in *The Golden Bowl,* the analyst channels his fascination with ethnic variety into a passion for cataloguing and preserving the various human "types," a term he employs "for easy convenience and not in respect to its indicating marked variety" (126). The variety of ethnic "types" is specifically unmarked throughout the city, where "the striking thing, and the beguiling, was always the manner in which figure after figure and face after face already betrayed the common consequence and action of their whereabouts" (126). The homogenizing effect of American culture, according to James, robs the alien of his or her ethnic distinctness almost from the moment of arrival, as if the Italian, Jew, or Irishman were "glazed with some mixture, of indescribable hue and consistency . . . that might have been applied . . . by a huge white-washing brush" (127).

The ethnic caricaturist's pen, whether it is wielded by Henry James or by E. W. Kemble, counters the effect of this whitewashing brush by exaggerating the physiognomic, gestural, and behavioral clichés upon which popular assumptions about ethnic identity rest. Indeed, Kemble's illustrations of "Xerky" in *A Coon Alphabet,* an unlikely companion to *The American Scene,* strike a decidedly Jamesian note on the alien subject's desire to erase the traces of ethnic origin (figures 3.1 and 3.2). The second image in the sequence, which represents the fulfillment of Xerky's wish to become white, would have appealed to James for its assertion that whitewash is powerless to alter or blur the exaggerated contours of ethnic difference. Kemble is characteristically shrewd in allowing the physiognomic tokens of

FIGURES 3.1–2. E. W. Kemble, *A Coon Alphabet*
(New York: R. H. Russell, 1899).

Xerky's "coon" identity—the grossly swollen lips, flattened nose, and sagging white eyes of figure 3.1—to show clearly through his racial disguise in the second illustration, marking him as an unalterable alien and the victim of a fruitless desire. The puckish hound, whose droopy features at first suggest a resemblance with his master, sits comfortably with a wide grin on his face in the sequel, participating in the viewer's awakened enjoyment at the spectacle of failed racial masquerade.

Kemble's images were a regular feature in middle-brow illustrated magazines like *Century*, the same magazines that published much of James's work and that he claimed to dislike. Reacting to the influence of contemporary magazines on the literary culture of his time, he complained about the "'picture-book' quality" of recent British and American prose and sought to distinguish his own writing from the "powerless" journalistic discourse of facts, pictures, and statistics.[2] The analyst of *The American Scene,* left momentarily speechless by the "shabby and sordid" cultural atmosphere of rural South Carolina, disparages the social drama by explaining that it was "as interesting, probably, as a 'short story' in one of the slangy dialects promoted by the illustrated monthly magazines" (397). Resolved at every opportunity to distinguish his super-fine impressions from the stark lines of the illustrator and the bogus science of the genealogist, he strains—at times awkwardly—to minimize and control the pictorial dimension of his art. Finding nothing to awaken his imagination during a walk in Baltimore, he is surprised to discover that his impression has fixed itself "by a wild logic of its own . . ., so that mine [my slate], by my walk's end, instead of a show of neat ciphering, exhibited simply a bold drawn image—which had the merit moreover of not being in the least a caricature" (308–9).

The Jamesian analyst repeatedly offers this self-description, juxtaposing his acute literary sensibility against the popular and banal milieu of illustration, which reaches its lowest form in the calculated distortions of journalistic caricature. Yet such overstated assertions of aesthetic privilege constitute a form of tongue-in-cheek engagement with the art of comic typification, which consistently informs James's rendering of American ethnic diversity at the turn of the century.[3] In fact, James professed deep admiration for the interplay of literary and graphic caricatures in the novels of Dickens and Thackeray, developing a taste for comic representation that later expressed itself in laudatory essays on Daumier and the great *Punch* caricaturist, Du Maurier, whom James recruited to illustrate *Washington*

Square.[4] "It is true," he admitted in *Picture and Text,* an 1893 collection of essays on artists and illustrators, "that what the verbal artist would like to do would be to find out the secret of the pictorial, to drink at the same fountain."[5] For all his coy efforts to deny an association with the "slangy" illustrated monthly magazines, the verbal artist does exactly this during those claustrophobic moments in *The American Scene,* when the "wild logic" of the "bold drawn image" asserts itself against the presence of alienism.

James's verbal caricatures may have contributed to a burgeoning nativist discourse at the turn of the century, but he did not understand his efforts in this way at all. In fact, his racialized critique of modern America invests exaggerated ethnic clichés with a surprising measure of cultural value, as if the richness of "type," should it become discernible, might serve to redeem the bland "sauce of New York." Attending an utterly conventional sentimental drama at the Bowery Theater, he observes that "in any attempt to render life," members of the older societies possess an "instinct of keeping closer" to what is real. "Yet here was my house full of foreigners, physiognomically branded as such, confronted with our pale poetic—fairly caught for schooling in our art of making the best of it" (231). Aligning his own art with that of the older societies, James laments the loss of native instinct in New York's recent immigrants, who appear regrettably eager to embrace the "pale poetic" of their adopted land. As this reference to complexion implies, America's makeshift aesthetic values threaten to absorb the very physiognomic qualities that produce, for the moment, an impression of ethnic diversity in the Bowery audience, an audience provisionally "branded" with the marks of ethnic origin and yet recklessly prone to assimilation. Proposing to recover the ethnic integrity of his subjects, the analyst wanders the streets of lower Manhattan's Italian neighborhoods like a naturalist in search of a more precise terminology for the categorization of distinct species. Noting the ubiquitous fire escapes that cover the tenement exteriors, he writes that "the appearance to which they most conduce is that of the spaciously organized cages for the nimbler class of animals in some great zoological garden. This general analogy is irresistible—it seems to offer, in each district, a little world of bars and perches and swings for human squirrels and monkeys" (134).

This descriptive logic operates as a perverse form of praise for groups that have preserved their "race-quality," despite the homogenizing effect of New York. The analyst explains that the American

Jew is "more savingly possessed of everything that is in him, than any other human, noted at random," because the "strength of the race permits of the chopping into myriads of fine fragments" without the loss of racial particularity (132). Of course, the "intensity of the Jewish aspect" is notably enviable from the point of view of the prodigal American writer, whose anxieties over personal dispossession and cultural dissipation color every page of *The American Scene* (132). On the other hand, the figure James devises to illustrate his conception of the "savingly possessed" Jewish Diaspora has the effect of dehumanizing, and thus dispossessing, the very subjects it is meant to praise. Because of their "unsurpassed strength," New York's Jews resemble "small strange animals, known to natural history, snakes or worms, I believe, who, when cut into pieces, wriggle away contentedly and live in the snippet as completely as in the whole" (132).

Clearly this sort of ethnic imagery puts the analyst back in possession of the scene, even as it concedes "the Hebrew conquest of New York" (132). Graphic caricatures of the period hinge on the same duality, revealing the razor-toting "coon" to be capable of violence only to himself or his own kind, exposing the savage Indian as nothing but a cowardly degenerate (figures 3.3 and 3.4). As with James's figure of the worm-like American Jew, the specter of alien potency is indulged, only to be contained in graphic gestures that make the ethnic subject childlike, feminine, or inhuman. The widespread practice of ethnic caricature in late nineteenth-century America originates with this impulse to "beguile" the bourgeois self into a Jamesian sense of "possession." For James himself, it is "an art to be cultivated," as he explains in a demanding passage:

> This sense of dispossession, to be brief about it, haunted me so, I was to feel, in the New York streets and in the packed trajectiles to which one clingingly appeals from the streets, just as one tumbles back into the streets in appalled reaction from *them,* that the art of beguiling or duping it became an art to be cultivated—though the fond alternative vision was never long to be obscured, the imagination, exasperated to envy, of the ideal, in the order in question; of the luxury of some such close and sweet and *whole* national consciousness as that of the Switzer and the Scot. (86)

To fabricate some alternative to a "*whole* national consciousness," and to guarantee the integrity of his own identity in the face

FIGURE 3.3. *Judge* 25 (November 1893): 322.

FIGURE 3.4. *Judge* 15 (November 1888): 107.

of persistent alien encroachments, the Jamesian analyst becomes a caricaturist, a specialist at "beguiling or duping" the accumulated xenophobic anxieties that plague his impressions of America. But to register only the defensive function of "the bold drawn image" is to underrate the complexity of James's relation to the popular art of ethnic misrepresentation. As Ross Posnock has argued so convincingly in *The Trial of Curiosity* and elsewhere, the zoological specimens of *The American Scene*—monkeys, squirrels, fish, and worms—emerge as uncanny points of identification for the analyst, whose "disgust," according to Posnock, occurs "within a frame of acceptance" and expresses an "unflinching affinity with the alien."[6] The Jew or Italian who projects a "note of settled possession" in his adopted home throws the analyst into a corresponding state of "*un*-settled possession," an unstable, hyphenated, postnational situation that is as liberating for the Jamesian analyst as it is unnerving. Indeed, for all the Anglo-American fervor that apparently animates his descriptions of outsiders, James was profoundly skeptical of static conceptions of national identity advocated by some of his most outspoken contemporaries, such as Theodore Roosevelt, who touted "pure Americanism" as a remedy for the diluting force of alienism.[7] James's critique of American culture at the turn of the century professes an alternative model of cosmopolitan identity, a model expressed in the paradox of the "alien" who is somehow exquisitely "at home." In exaggerating the foreignness of the ethnic subject according to the conventions of graphic caricature—such that the alien's "home" comes to resemble an aquarium or a cage—the analyst merely accentuates the paradox of his own status as a "restored absentee," a figure who is himself, according to Peter Conn, "the most patently ubiquitous of the aliens" to be found in New York's crowded streets.[8]

"If I had had time to become almost as 'fresh' as an inquiring stranger," the analyst declares at the beginning of *The American Scene*, "I had not . . . had enough to cease to be, or at least feel, as acute as an initiated native" (1). Searching out a liminal position somewhere between the overdetermined extremes of alienism and Americanism, the restless analyst portrays himself as another sort of grotesque, a free-floating aesthete who—like the "ubiquitous alien"—has been "amputated of half of my history" (91). Posnock notes that James's ambivalent movement between "revulsion" and "subterranean identification" with the alien produces a "third term," the "perpetually provisional" stance of the narrator, whose oxymoronic predicament conveys the essence of James's subtle approach to cultural critique.⁹ Ethnic caricature, among the most abhorrent devices of American chauvinism, participates in this critique by enabling James to assert and to complicate his "supreme relation" to America simultaneously.

This process of negotiating one's relation to America by way of the caricatured image takes a number of forms in *The American Scene*. After leaving the crowded neighborhoods of New York, where "the treasures of type" require exaggerated emphasis, the analyst boards a southbound train and immediately finds himself isolated from the scene of his impressions by the "inordinate luxury" of "a cushioned and kitchened Pullman" (398). No longer threatened by the teeming streets and railways of Manhattan, he now struggles to overcome the "awful modern privilege of this detached yet concentrated stare at the misery of subject populations" (397). His impressions disabled by the extremity of his detachment, in contrast to the uncomfortable intimacy of New York, James again invokes ethnic caricature to repair the analyst's appropriate relation to his subject. Having observed "a group of tatterdemalion darkies" while they "lounged and sunned themselves" like exotic reptiles at the depot, he studies the forms and features of black pedestrians as the train passes, concluding that "they obviously, they notoriously, didn't care for themselves" (375, 398). "It was a monstrous thing," James admits from his comfortable seat, "to deny to so many groups of one's fellow-creatures any claim to a 'personality'; but this was in truth what one was perpetually doing" (398).

Kenneth Warren and others have objected to James's dehumanizing imagery in this passage, which clearly draws on the conventions of "coon" comedy to depict African Americans as thoughtless reptiles.¹⁰ Indeed, Kemble was particularly adept at suggesting a physiognomic analogy between his "coon" characters and alligators, crocodiles, and frogs. Such objections are entirely valid, and yet it is worth noticing that caricature stigmatizes the detached aestheticism of the analyst in this scene as effectively as it evokes the carelessness of his black subjects. Immersed in the "inordinate luxury" of the Pullman car, James portrays himself with exaggerated emphasis as a modern American pasha, adopting an almost comical tone of self-aggrandizement to announce that "it was only the restless analyst himself who cared—and enough, after all, he finally felt, to make up for other deficiencies" (398). Caricature here works in two directions at once to emphasize the paralyzing gulf that separates an absurdly

THE PROFESSOR IS IMPRESSED BY THE APE'S BUMP OF LAN-
GUAGE, AND DECIDES TO MAKE RESEARCHES ON THE FIELD.

ARRIVING ON AFRICA'S SOIL, HE IS STRUCK WITH THE INTEL-
LIGENCE DISPLAYED BY A SUBJECT.

FIGURES 3.5–11. *Life* 24
(Aug. 30, 1894): 138–40.

magnanimous analyst from the depraved reptiles who bask like lazy
vermin in the sun. James develops such disturbing asymmetries to
dramatize his larger complaint with American culture at the turn of
the century, a culture that, in his view, denies the sensitive observer
the true, rather than "inordinate," luxury of an appropriate relation
to experience. Finding himself alternately much too close or much
too far from the social object at hand, he deploys caricature to nego-
tiate a viable—and consistently problematic—subject position. Beguiling himself into a sense of detachment or intimacy, as the situation demands, the analyst fashions an exaggerated and frequently
comical image of himself as, in Thomas Peyser's words, "one tangled
with the alien."[11]

The comic papers of James's period regularly featured a parallel
form of critique. Much as James employed caricature as a reflexive
device, capable of denaturalizing his own claims to ethnic and cultural privilege, magazines such as *Life* and *Puck* often redirected the
usual force of ethnic misrepresentation by poking innocent fun at
the foibles of the "dominant" race. A representative series of illustrations in *Life* depicts a professor of phrenology examining the skull of
an ape, which impresses him with the size of its "bump of language"
(figures 3.5, 3.6, 3.7, 3.8, 3.9, 3.10, and 3.11). Operating on an assumption shared by phrenologists and caricaturists alike—the assumption
that exterior dimensions of the face and skull connote attributes of
temperament and intellect—the professor travels to Africa in search
of intelligent life. There he discovers a subject with "a wonderful tal-

WHO RESPONDS TO HIS SALUTATIONS

AND DISPLAYS A WONDERFUL TALENT FOR MIMICRY.

WHEREUPON THE PROFESSOR DECIDES TO TAKE THE INTELLIGENT SUBJECT BACK WITH HIM TO CIVILIZATION.

BUT HIS PLANS ARE FOILED,

AND A NUMBER OF GENIAL APES ARE NOW ADVANCING A THEORY THAT MONKEY IS DERIVED FROM MAN.

ent for mimicry," a talent so advanced that the ape soon takes control of the situation, confirming the professor's hypothesis about simian intelligence, while turning the usual account of human evolution on its head. Of course, the professor's antics from the first image to the last have betrayed him as a kind of intellectual savage long before his plans have been "foiled" by an unexpectedly "civilized" subject. Caricature here and in *The American Scene* destabilizes ethnic hierarchies in the act of exaggerating their claims to cultural authority, revealing the caricaturist as a victim of his own mode of calculated misrepresentation.

For all their bluntness as instruments of systemic condescension, illustrations of ethnic subjects often focused explicitly on this reflexive feature of the caricatured image. An 1883 illustration in *Life*, for example, turns the era's aggressively dehumanizing racial imagery against the parent culture by aligning the images of a cigar store Indian, an Irish street cleaner, and a foppishly dressed American gentleman (figure 3.12). The arrangement of these figures from background to foreground—and the corresponding discrepancy in their proportions—evokes another Darwinist account of man's gradual ascent from savagery to civilization, a familiar motif in American ethnic caricature. Yet while the sketch's evolutionary logic appears to guarantee the white man's place at the top of a hierarchy of ethnic types, the caption "Three of a Kind" insists on reading differences of physiognomy, dress, and occupation—differences that constitute the social hierarchy—as insignificant. Hopelessly "tangled with the alien," like James's ubiquitous analyst, the white man of fashion forfeits his claim to social prestige by revealing himself as merely another reified principle of ethnic identity.

The *Life* illustration toys with another subversive idea, namely that by exchanging their broom and tomahawk for a fashionable cane, the Irishman and the wooden Indian can assume a new ethnic identity altogether, a possibility that is imperfectly discouraged by their grossly distended facial features. Caricatures of the period generally squash this illicit fantasy, preferring to celebrate the predictable failure of every imaginable effort at ethnic uplift, assimilation, or disguise. Yet in exaggerating the physiognomic, gestural, and cultural stigmas that make ethnic identity irreversible, the caricaturist inevitably calls attention to their status as culturally mediated symbols, reintroducing the troublesome possibility that ethnic identity may be nothing more than a performance.

THREE OF A KIND.

FIGURE 3.12. *Life* 2
(August 1883): 72.

James would have found little entertainment in *Life*'s many-
layered satire, but the head-on collision of these irreconcilable conceptions human identity—one that understands ethnicity as a symbolic mask worn by an essentially independent individual, another
that interprets every individual through the lens of ethnic origin—
produces a tension that is as much a feature of late nineteenth-
century caricature as it is of the Jamesian text. One critic, Martha
Banta, has made this connection explicit by situating James at the
margins of a robust visual culture that excelled in addressing complex anxieties over racial and national identity through graphic satire
and caricature. It is unlikely that an issue of *Life* magazine ever
crossed the threshold of James's study, and yet Banta hints at an intriguing parallel when she compares *Life*'s aggressively condescending treatment of Native Americans with James's characterization of
Prince Amerigo, the irreparable Italian nobleman of *The Golden
Bowl.* Contemplating the viability of marriages between white

American women and Native American males in an 1891 editorial, *Life* expressed an ostensibly liberal view:

> Our estimate of the negro and the Indian races is that they are both inferior, but the inferiority of the Indian, which shows in his inaptitude for civilized life and unwillingness to work, has always inspired more or less of our respect. We often feel about him . . . that he has the feelings of a gentleman, and our sentiments toward him take the form of sympathy for him as a person who has known better days.[12]

With its calculated blend of condescension and approval of native "inferiority," the editorial condones the intermarriage of white women to Indian men in principle, noting that "the American girl has shown that she likes novelty in a husband, and why should a chief be less acceptable than an Italian prince?"[13] In the course of her elaborate and nuanced discussion of *Life*'s racial attitudes, Banta finds it necessary to do little more than emphasize the final twelve words of this sentence to suggest a parallel with *The Golden Bowl*, which she describes as a novel in which "the devoted American father encourages his daughter to enter upon an intercultural marriage with an Italian nobleman whose past is marked by barbarities of history, refinement of manners, and the incapacity to earn his own way."[14] Drawing from the language of the editorial to complete her synopsis of the novel, she concludes that "[a]s a happy result" of intermarriage, "'the Indian question would be solved,' and one more imported floater absorbed into the ruling social system."[15]

Banta pursues her primary subject in another direction, but her abbreviated account begins to suggest that *Life* and other periodicals that featured ethnic caricature expressed what might be considered a Jamesian form of ambivalence over the role of ethnicity in the structure of identity. Or, to give the same point a different emphasis, James's representation of ethnicity in *The Golden Bowl* and elsewhere is surprisingly in tune with the "coon era"'s popular discourse of ethnic caricature. The basic contours of this discourse are by now familiar: the ethnic identity of the Irishman, the Jew, the Indian, or the African American was easily conveyed by an exaggerated physical stigma, a permanent mark that denoted a set of culturally agreed upon social pathologies, such as intemperance, avarice, savagery, or laziness. Yet the very form of ethnic caricature—its exaggerated emphasis on the subject's purported deviation from physical and social norms—made such markers ridiculous and thus inherently unstable, such that ethnic identities were often represented as arbitrarily interchangeable. The entertainment value of late-nineteenth-century ethnic caricatures hinged on this clumsy juxtaposition of two very different accounts of identity, one that generates humor by representing ethnicity as a fixed and limiting condition, another that treats "blood" as a laughable fiction. By its very nature, comic typification suggests an awkward tension between these competing ideas, both of which are clearly discernable in *Life*'s endorsement of intermarriage between white women and native men. Indeed, the Indian chief's ethnically specific brand of "inferiority," his "inaptitude for civilized life and unwillingness to work," is only emphasized by the assertion that he is as suitable for marriage as an Italian Prince. Ethnicity is a fungible category, the editorial seems to say, and yet only by remembering the Indian's irreversible alienness can we acknowledge his ostensible sameness.

This curiously circular logic is at work in Frederick Opper's "A Miraculous Metamorphosis; or, Bridget's Sudden Rise." The presence of a police officer comfortably seated in Bridget's American kitchen, in contrast to the eviction notice that looms over her Irish shanty in the opening image, would appear to suggest that immigration entails a significant readjustment in arrangements of power and authority (figures 3.13 and 3.14). It might furthermore be observed that Bridget's posture has become more defiant and her expression more assertive with her "sudden rise" in social stature. Yet despite her improved company and external surroundings, including a slim waistline and a fashionable costume, the Irish drudge still stares vacantly into the symbol of her permanent domestic routine. The exchange of a savage looking mother and a skinny pig in the first illustration for a Murray Hill housewife and a portly policeman in the second has done little to soften Bridget's masculine features or to alter her occupation, which are reproduced in a mirror image to signify the sameness of her new existence in New York. One is left to ponder whether the illustration's title is hyperbolic—suggesting that identity is ethnic and thus impervious to the effects of a new environment—or descriptive—implying that the human self is discrete, autonomous, and susceptible to "miraculous metamorphosis." The illustration raises this question only to withhold its solution behind Bridget's ambiguous, frozen stare.

The comic interest of Opper's illustration stems neither from its perfectly standard representation of Irish physiognomy nor from a simple assertion of social advantages available to Americans. What

makes the image visually compelling, rather, is its uncertain commitment to the very possibility of metamorphosis, its presumption that ethnicity can be understood as at once a fixed condition and an arbitrary disguise. Of course, James's fiction rarely stoops to notice suburban life in neighborhoods such as Murray Hill, and yet the illustration's playful questioning of Bridget's transformation is suggestive of the Jamesian analyst's own predicament as the "perpetually provisional" observer of *The American Scene*, a hybrid figure who is neither "as fresh as an inquiring stranger" nor "as acute as an initiated native." I have already discussed James's ambivalent excursions into the zoological ghettos of New York as a form of fieldwork for the literary ethnologist whose meditations on ethnic variety help to assuage nativist fears of dispossession, even as they articulate a cosmopolitan notion of identity. Sara Blair has written with great insight on the closely related interplay between a "natural" conception of self and "the power of type" in *The Princess Casamassima*, raising concerns that unfold even more suggestively in her discussion of Miriam Rooth, the Jewish heroine of *The Tragic Muse*.[16] But as Martha Banta intuits in *Barbarous Intercourse*, James's most searching application of the logic of ethnic caricature to questions of identity occurs in his last and, in many respects, greatest novel, *The Golden Bowl*.

The novel's opening paragraphs frame a question that will occupy nearly eight hundred pages of Jamesian character analysis, a question handled more abruptly, if not more conclusively, in countless caricatures of the period: will Prince Amerigo's marriage to an American heiress produce a "miraculous metamorphosis," or is his identity inseparable from the ethnic aura that pervades "his whole person," filling even his clothes with an "inexpungable scent."[17] The Italian prince embarks on his romantic experiment with Maggie Verver in an entrepreneurial spirit, determined to "contradict, and even if need be flatly dishonour" the "antenatal history" that expresses itself in Amerigo's stereotypical features, from his perpetually over-active hands to the curly dark hair on his head, which "might have been steeped . . . in some chemical bath" (1:16). For all the sincerity of his "desire for some new history," however, Amerigo cautiously acknowledges that he is "somehow full of his race," and he worries that traces of its legacy will not be so easily removed (1:16). Warning Maggie that she "really know[s] nothing" about his complicated predicament—his uncertain relation to an ethnic past and to a hypothetical American future—he explains to her: "There are two parts of me. . . . One that is made up of the history, the doings, the marriages, the crimes, the follies, the boundless *bêtises* of other people. . . . But there's another part, very much smaller, doubtless, which, such as it is, represents my single self, the unknown, unimportant—unimportant save to *you*—personal quantity. About this you've found out nothing" (1:9).

Maggie's glib rejoinder—"Luckily, my dear"—underscores her faith that Amerigo's "personal quantity," the part of his identity that bears no relation to his ancient pedigree, is not Italian. She insists that the "follies and the crimes" of his infamous family history contribute to his value as "a rarity, an object of beauty, an object of price," and she sensibly asks where the Prince would be without his ethnic past (1:9–10). Yet Maggie's confidence that her own marriage is something other than a repetition of past iniquities rests on her belief that a perfect distinction can be drawn between the ethnic aspect of Amerigo's identity, which fills the annals of the public library, and the "single self" that remains "unknown" even to her. "Oh I'm not afraid of history," she remarks in one of many confident declarations that "sweetened the waters in which he now floated, tinted them as by the action of some essence, poured from a gold-topped phial for making one's bath aromatic" (1:9–10). The waters in which Amerigo floats during the hours before his attempted metamorphosis are made bitter by his consciousness of "how little one of his race could escape after all from history" (1:10). Into these waters Maggie "scattered, on occasion, her exquisite coloring drops," little remarks that convey her faith in a raceless "essence" of personality underlying Amerigo's Italian identity (1:10). Ethnicity almost disappears as a feature of the self in the aromatic solution of their intimacy, a magical effect of the "coloring drops" that James represents as significantly colorless. "They were of the colour—of what on earth? of what but the extraordinary American good faith? They were of the colour of her innocence, and yet at the same time of her imagination, with which their relation, his and these people's, was all suffused." (1:10)

Of course, the perfumed prenuptial bath in which Maggie attempts to cleanse her betrothed of his ethnic quality serves only to disguise Amerigo's ancestral gift for Machiavellian intrigue, which surfaces in force even before the moment of their marriage. With the arrival of his former lover, Charlotte Stant, the Prince experiences what ethnologists of the period would have described as a "reversion to type," a return of the savage instincts that define a specific ethnic group.[18] Years earlier, adopting the analyst's role in an essay on Italian ways, James had compiled a list of attributes belonging to the Venetian "race," a list that reads strangely like an indictment against the duplicitous Prince: the Venetian "hasn't a genius for stiff morality. . . . It scruples but scantly to represent the false as the true. . . . It has been accused further of loving if not too well at least too often."[19] Under the cover of Maggie's pervasive naïveté, the Prince gradually emerges as what he has been all along, an unreconstructed Italian and an ethnic type of the most predictable sort, one whose "remarkable powers of assimilation" serve only to mask his genetic allegiance to a degenerate race. His story is the story of Kemble's "coons," those tragic racial masqueraders whose failure to transcend the limiting conditions of race provided such endless opportunities for entertainment in magazines, sketchbooks, and illustrated novels of the era. As Jonathan Freedman has explained, Amerigo's "failure to ameliorate the racially coded vices" that define his character produces "an image of the unassimilated, unassimilable alien," "a noble, indeed thoroughly distinguished version of that figure, but one whose full integration into the Anglo-Saxon sphere is at least as questionable as that of the eastern European Jews who were entering London's East End or New York's Lower East Side in such extraordinary numbers at that very moment."[20]

Amerigo's inability to shed his racial attributes suggests that the sources of identity lie beyond the self, in the public sphere of history, tradition, and physiognomy. Like the amateur ethnologists in the graphic departments at *Puck* and *Judge,* James implies that the individual is always fundamentally true to type, that Maggie can learn all she needs to know about her husband's "single self" by consulting the written history of his notorious race. Yet if Amerigo's botched attempt at assimilation demonstrates that blood will tell, the novel's American characters support an entirely different conception of identity. Charlotte at one point boasts of her "Anglo-Saxon blood," but the Prince aptly corrects her by exclaiming, "Blood? . . . You've that of every race. . . . You're terrible" (1:362). Indeed, Amerigo feels separated from his new American relatives by "an abyss of divergence," an abyss that connotes more than the difference between Anglo-Saxon and Italian blood, for the Americans in *The Golden Bowl* exemplify a condition of racial truancy (1:310). Amerigo's ethnic origin "sticks out" of his exquisitely typical profile, whereas Mr. Verver's American face is "colourless," "*clear,* and in this manner somewhat resembled a small decent room, clean-swept and unencumbered with furniture" (1:9, 1:170). Charlotte's "race-quality" is equally difficult to "disembroil," according to the narrator, who explains that her uncanny fluency in foreign tongues, coupled with "her solitude, her want of means," her "want of ramifications," produces the impression of "an odd precious neutrality," a sense of detachment from any ethnic, cultural, or familial origin (1:54). Charlotte "hasn't a creature in the world," only "distant relations," according to Maggie, who shares Fanny Assingham's opinion that Miss Stant's striking charisma originates in the fact that "she ha[s] only to be what she is—and to be it all round" (1:180, 1:195). Bewildered by a structure of identity that he cannot understand, much less emulate, the Prince conjectures that Charlotte and the Ververs are "of the same race . . . of the same general tradition and education, of the same moral paste" (1:310). But this attempt to fit the Americans into an ethnic mold is another sign of Amerigo's confusion, for "the race of the Ververs," as Thomas Peyser explains, "is an emptiness, pure potentiality, nothing as yet."[21]

Even when the novel's Americans lay claim to a symbolic ethnic origin, as when Maggie compares her situation to that of "some Indian squaw," the analogy serves to accentuate rather than to ameliorate a condition of ethnic migrancy and instability (2:323). Unlike the Prince, who confronts the crisis in their marital relation by remaining "as fixed in his place as some statue of one of his forefathers," Maggie finds it necessary, like her imaginary ancestress, to "move indefatigably" through some uncharted territory that "would have been sought in vain on the most rudimentary map of the social relations" (2:324). "It was strange, if one had gone into it," exclaims the narrator, "but such a place as Amerigo's was like something made for him beforehand by innumerable facts . . . made by ancestors, examples, traditions, habits; while Maggie's own had come to show simply as that improvised 'post'—a post of the kind spoken of as advanced—with which she was to have found herself connected in the fashion of a settler or a trader in a new country; in the likeness even of some Indian squaw with a papoose on her back and barbarous beadwork to sell" (2:323–24).

Mark Seltzer has discussed this curious linkage of the colonizing "settler" or "trader" with the colonized squaw as evidence that Maggie deploys power and passivity together as "the double surface of a single strategy."[22] Seltzer's insight might be redirected toward a related observation that the passage makes Maggie's race indistinguishable from her racelessness, for James here employs a static ethnic image—the image of a symbolic American ethnicity—to evoke Maggie's improvisational condition. Whereas "innumerable facts" of ancestry and tradition determine in advance the Prince's fixed position in the world and in their relationship, Maggie's racial heritage, her imagined connection to an ethnic source, only underscores her lack of a permanent "place." James deploys the boomerang logic of ethnic caricature in this scene with all the finesse regularly demonstrated by *Life's* editorial staff, allowing the enigmatic "Indian squaw" to operate simultaneously as an explanation and a disavowal of ethnic origin.

Of all the unhappy marriages in James's fiction, this one is perhaps the most understandable. In Prince Amerigo and his wife, the novel offers two radically opposed and, for James, equally untenable, models of identity: the self as a thoroughly historical entity that is stationary and defined by an ethnic principle, and the self as a strictly private phenomenon, destined "to move indefatigably," capable of "miraculous metamorphosis," unencumbered by anything beyond itself. As Jonathan Freedman has explained, "both wife and husband must be altered in order to produce a new order—a new marital, a new genetic, and thus ultimately a new racial order—of identity."[23] The novel moves uncertainly toward such a mutual transformation as Maggie learns to manipulate others by mastering, according to Freedman, "precisely those elements of the Prince's character that are most alien to her, and most race-specific to him," whereas Amerigo gradually develops something resembling an Anglo-American conscience.[24] Yet James is characteristically ambiguous about the viability of the new order of identity that may be signified by the couple's closing embrace, which is fraught with tension and misunderstanding. One is tempted to speculate that Maggie's successful rehabilitation of their relationship has inspired a delicate balance between the "fixed" ethnicity of the Prince and her own "improvised" Americanness, two seemingly irreconcilable attitudes that combine in the novel's closing scene to suggest a marital version of the "perpetually provisional" stance of the analyst in *The American Scene*. Yet just as the terms of this oxymoronic pairing refuse to dissolve into one another, the two young people remain tensely divided, even in the act of their final embrace. Maggie's inscrutable comment—"That's our help, you see"—offered ostensibly to clarify her equally cryptic observation that Charlotte is "too splendid," throws the Prince into a state of confusion:

It kept him before her therefore, taking in—or trying to—what she so wonderfully gave. He tried, too clearly, to please her—to meet her in her own way; but with the result only that, close to her, her face kept before him, his hands holding her shoulders, his whole act enclosing her, he presently echoed: "'See'? I see nothing but *you*." And the truth of it had with this force after a moment so strangely lighted his eyes that as for pity and dread of them she buried her own in his breast. (2:368–69)

Two of the novel's shrewdest readers concur that James is groping here for a means of representing the transcendence of race as a category of identity. For Peyser, the novel assuages James's "fear of racial determinism" by gesturing toward a cosmopolitan utopia, a raceless world-community signified by Maggie's reconstructed marriage, which "heralds the birth of the race that overcomes race."[25] Freedman also maintains that Maggie's triumph leaves the Prince "purged of racial characteristics," for the hand that embraces her on the novel's final page "is no longer given a racial identification or appellation."[26] Moreover, Freedman explains that the ambiguity of the closing scene "seems to signify both that the novel understands the necessity of the new order of possibility represented by the newly established identity of the Prince and that it understands as well what this new order of possibility implies: a transcendence of the very notion of race that the novel has itself, until this moment, relied upon." The curious play of submission and dominance, of "pity and dread," that characterizes the final lines demonstrates, for Freedman, "the extent of James's imaginative failure," for "it shows that he has no means of imagining and picturing this new order of identity, no terms for encompassing the new form of identity that this triad, Maggie, the Prince, and the Principino, will create."[27]

I have quoted Peyser and Freedman at such length because I think they are right in almost every respect. The novel does imagine a radical process of assimilation that seems designed to produce the conditions for an entirely new order of identity. Yet much as Bridget's Irishness remains a central fact of her "new" existence in New York, race persists as a defining feature of the hyphenated, complex identities that are produced through the novel's torturous process of rehabilitation. Maggie must cultivate a Machiavellian awareness of the convoluted social relations that structure her world, a form of awareness that is alien to her Emersonian understanding of the self as a monadic, autonomous, essentially private entity. The Prince, by contrast, must make room for the "single self" or "personal quantity" that his racially charged Italian constitution has all along seemed to preclude. The "new order of identity" that both characters point toward, and that their offspring intends to signify, does not represent "a transcendence of the very notion of race," nor does it herald "the birth of the race that overcomes race." Indeed, the strangely deracinated and incestuous Ververs appear to have accomplished this transcendence at the outset, and James makes it clear that their disengaged connoisseurship, no less than Amerigo's Italian promiscuity, is responsible for the breakdown of marital intimacy and procreative power that the novel seeks to mend. In short, characters in the novel possess alternately too much race or too little, and either condition produces a grotesque figure for identity. James's exquisitely irresolute ending refuses either to envision a tidy synthesis or to disentangle the oxymoronic pairings—"restored absentee," "settled dispossession"—that constitute his understanding of the self in its perpetual relation to others, the self as simultaneously a unique, organic phenomenon and a social construct. The ambiguously reunited couple, like the imperfect golden bowl, represents not an "imaginative failure" on James's part, but a new order of "personality" based on the premise that, as Theodore Adorno would explain, "the identity of the self and its alienation are companions from the beginning."[28]

James's most compact image for this paradoxical structure of identity occurs in his representation of the novel's Jews, the antiquarian merchants who preside over *The Golden Bowl*'s two marriages with the solemnity of "some mystic rite of old Jewry" (1:216). Freedman has argued so effectively for the thematic significance of these shadowy figures that I will not press the point, except to suggest that both characters embody the paradox that underlies the central action of the novel, namely the idea that identity might be at once public and private, fixed and in motion, ethnic and unique.[29] While Maggie and the Prince inch their way toward a condition of identity *possibly* sympathetic to such tense pairings, the novel's Jews already blend strict conformity to type with an entrepreneurial spirit that rivals Adam Verver's own. The "overdeveloped proboscis" of *The American Scene* reappears in the predictably "impersonal old noses" of the Gutermann-Seuss children, who are unquestionably marked by inflexible racial characteristics. But the antique dealer creates an odd impression of detachment from his numerous progeny, appearing "to the casual eye" as "a mere smart and shining youth of less than thirty summers," and it is only Charlotte's keen eye for racial "types" that reconnects him to an ethnic origin (1:213). The novel's other antiquarian, the "swindling little Jew" who demands a high price for his fractured relic, effortlessly overrides his pronounced "race-quality" in revealing to Maggie the symbolic flaw that mars both the bowl and her marriage (1:359). If the shop keeper's physiognomy and mannerisms label him as a "horrid little beast," his unexpected command of Italian suggests that the Jew is at the same time both a knowable ethnic epitome and an oddly amorphous cultural chameleon (2:197). Like the "small strange animals" of New York's Jewish quarter, these internally paradoxical figures live "in the snippet as completely as in the whole," and their irreducible duality establishes the terms for the novel's central question of identity.

The novel's antiquarian traders present a special case for James, because he understands the Jew's cosmopolitanism as both an expression and a repudiation of "race-quality." Yet the same paradox of identity is a constitutive feature of the caricatured ethnic image more generally.[30] Indeed, Opper's representation of Bridget as an Irish-American takes the ambiguous hyphen in this construction as its theme, asking with James if it is possible to be fundamentally ethnic and improvisationally American at the same time. By virtue of its very form, the exaggerated ethnic image fixes identity according to inflexible genetic categories, even as it reduces its subject to a set of arbitrary symbolic components. Ethnic caricature appeals to James for its economical expression of this internal contradiction.

James has been justly challenged for his nativist and anti-Semitic sensibilities, and indeed he often cast himself in the role of an Anglo-American cultural steward, poised defensively against the incursion an alien menace. Caricature served him effectively in this mood, much as it served the period's journalistic illustrators as a means to define the boundaries of a privileged ethnic elite against the insistent presence of alienism. The defensive pose is a common rhetorical feature of *The American Scene,* where the analyst declares that the "honour" of the American "man of letters . . . sits astride of the consecrated English tradition," whereas "the dragon most rousing . . . the proper spirit of St. George, is just this immensity of the alien presence climbing higher and higher."[31] Envisioning himself as a mythical defender of race-specific Anglo-American cultural values, charging into battle astride the tradition of English literature, James appears to have foreclosed any possibility of "subterranean identification" with the terrifying "immensity of the alien presence." But the knight of deliverance is just as absurdly exaggerated as his ethnic adversary in this caricatured self-representation, and both figures are tied together, as Peyser explains, "in a definitional knot" that refuses to be undone.[32] Their endless altercation rages in and through Bridget's inscrutable expression, an expression reproduced on the distorted faces of immigrants and African Americans throughout the age of caricature. The Jamesian art of ethnic misrepresentation carries this mythic conflict into the most intimate phases of mental and emotional life, where the "definitional knot" becomes a basis for reconceptualizing identity in terms of a series of taut relationships between self and other, native and alien, private and public. Like the caricaturists of his era, the analyst plays his race card with brutal insensitivity, but this St. George never defeats the dragon of ethnicity, and their perpetual conflict animates a psychological drama that, for James, has no ending.

4
Edith Wharton's Flamboyant Copy

"I want the idols broken, but I want them broken by people who understand why they were made."
—Wharton notebook, Beinecke Library, Yale University.

Edith Wharton was an ambivalent anthropologist of manners. Her satires of elite social life in New York, Newport, and Europe delight in exposing the arbitrary nature of social forms that support a rigidly hierarchical class structure, but they do so from the point of view of one of those "people who understand" why such forms are necessary and remain, at some level, worth preserving. As Nancy Bentley explained, Wharton's immanent critique of the rituals that mystify and consolidate social privilege pursues a "double-strategy," one that finally affirms the very structures it purports to challenge.[1] The "novelist-ethnographer" betrays the fraud of elite social status in turn-of-the-century America, but the fact remains that, as Jack Stepney puts it in *The House of Mirth,* "we don't marry Rosedale in our family."[2]

An equally perverse ambivalence about the nature of class difference, ethnic identity, and social privilege informs the era's discourse of popular caricature, as the scandalous images in a contemporary sketchbook attest. The title of E. W. Kemble's 1899 collection *Coontown's 400* sought to poke fun at Caroline Jacob Astor's celebrated effort to address the social disorder of New York by conferring special status upon the city's most prominent families, who became known as the Astor Four Hundred.[3] This self-proclaimed aristocratic enclave was a favorite target of caricaturists, who lampooned the social ambitions of "the golden mien" with characteristic subtlety (figure 4.1). Kemble's outrageous images of New York's black upper crust belong to this genre of Hogarthian satire, which purports to champion middle-class values in defiance of the artificial social posturing

FIGURE 4.1. "The Golden Mien," *Life*, date unknown.

of institutions like the Four Hundred (figure 4.2). His pompous "coons" expose the fraud of social prestige when their hopeless imitation of leisure degenerates into hazardous slapstick comedy. But if Kemble's illustrations make sport of the hollow tokens of class distinction, they simultaneously work to consolidate social status by insinuating that a "coon," no matter what airs he may put on, always remains "nothin' but a coon."[4] Indeed, Kemble's satire of the Astor Four Hundred deploys a crude version of Wharton's "double-strategy," for the critique of an artificially rigid social structure operates in the context of exaggerated physiognomic evidence of class and ethnic permanence. Kemble might have wished to invert the terms of Wharton's tautological journal entry by asserting something like, "I want the idols preserved, but I want them preserved by people who know they are false," but the effect of such circular reasoning is the same in either case. The idiom through which this paradox makes itself felt in both *Coontown's 400* and *The House of Mirth* is the idiom of ethnic caricature.

Ethnic images of the sort that Kemble and his colleagues made famous consistently employ this curious logic, challenging the categories of class and ethnic organization in late nineteenth century America, only to underwrite their authority more firmly in the realm

FIGURE 4.2. E. W. Kemble, *Coontown's 400* (New York: Life Publishing, 1899).

of ethnic representation. In their crudest form, such images question the humanity of the ethnic subject, deploying caricature to blur the line between man and ape, even as they inscribe an ever more inflexible conceptual boundary between the "higher" and "lower" races (figure 4.3). If the didactic purposes of such illustrations are grossly plain, the editorial component of some caricatures betrays an almost schizophrenic attitude toward the ethnic subject's capacity for transformation, uplift, or assimilation. As John Appel has observed, demeaning images of the Jew were often paired with strikingly sympathetic commentary on the suitability of "the children of Israel" as American citizens.[5] "In spite of a few professional American Jew baiters, . . . the people of this country are very glad to welcome this addition to our population," crooned a *Puck* editorial, which accompanied an illustration of Uncle Sam as "The Modern Moses" (figure 4.4).[6] "We do not mean to say that they are the greatest race that ever existed, but they have many remarkable and admirable qualities." When the editor of the *Jewish Messenger* objected to the "shameful" tone of the illustration, *Puck* countered with a diatribe that effectively conveyed the paper's conflicted position on the functions of caricature in the representation of ethnic identity:

> We have no prejudice against the Jews or the Jewish religion, . . . no prejudice against the Irish or the Roman Catholics; and if mere caricature is objectionable, the Irish have surely much more reason to complain than the Jews, who have always found a champion in *Puck*. Our Hebrew friends must not be so sensitive; and, like sensible people as they are, must take a joke as their neighbors take one. If they do not wish to be made fun of, they should not intensify the traditional peculiarities that so often make them the subject of ridicule. They are clannish, and cling to their antiquated puerile Oriental customs and mummeries as a Chinaman clings to his pigtail. They should become Americans. Let them mix, marry and associate—we will not say with Christians, as there are few real Christians nowadays—but with non-Jews or Gentiles and get rid of the silly idea that their race and religion are immeasurably above all others. If this were done, there would, in time, be no more reason to caricature the peculiarities of a Jew, as a Jew, than of a Quaker, a Swedenborgian, a Shaker, or an Episcopalian.

This candid expression of what Appel calls *Puck's* "split-personality" insists that the "reason to caricature" the peculiarities of the Jew is that "puerile Oriental customs and mummeries," tokens of the Jew's ethnic identity, interfere with his total assimilation. Of course, the terms of this exaggerated characterization, like the graphic image to which it is linked, make total assimilation highly problematic by reinscribing precisely the same cultural and physiognomic markers of Jewishness that the *Puck* editorial considers dispensable, a paradox neatly appreciated in the *Jewish Messenger's* angry comment that in *Puck* "fun and ridicule are synonymous." The parenthetical dodge that invites Jews to "mix, marry and associate" with Gentiles, but not with "real Christians," reflects an equally ambivalent attitude toward

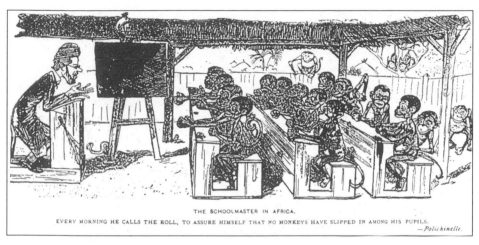

FIGURE 4.3. "The Schoolmaster in Africa," *Life* 29 (April 1897): 320.

FIGURE 4.4. "The Modern Moses," *Puck* (December 1881), reproduced in John J. Appel, "Jews in American Caricature: 1820–1914," *Jewish American History* 71 (September 1981): 103–33.

the ideology of the melting pot, suggesting once again that Edith Wharton's qualified social radicalism—her interest in seeing the idols destroyed and legitimized at the same time—might serve as an effective gloss on editorial policies governing the practice of ethnic caricature at the period's leading illustrated papers.

If *Puck* in this episode appears to hedge awkwardly on the question of total assimilation, offering outlandish images of the Jew as both an incitement to racial blending and as reassurance that no amount of blending can disguise Shylock, other *Puck* images confront the question more directly. A remarkable illustration from 1893, entitled "Looking Backward," depicts five wealthy Americans who stand poised to block the entrance of a newly arrived immigrant (figure 4.5). The hypocrisy of their xenophobic position is cleverly exposed on the opposite wall, where their shadows betray the stout Americans as relatively recent immigrants themselves. The image unquestionably challenges anti-immigrationist sentiment, which reached unprecedented levels during the 1890s as arrivals from Southern and Eastern Europe for the first time exceeded those from

FIGURE 4.5. Joseph Keppler, "Looking Backward," *Puck* (1893), reproduced in John J. Appel, "From Shanties to Lace Curtains: The Irish Image in Puck, 1876–1910," *Comparative Studies in Society and History* 13 (1971): 365–75.

the North. Yet if the image invites readers to place their faith in the transformative power of the American melting-pot, it also suggests that one's ethnic identity never really disappears. Caricature, according to *Puck's* editorial on Jewish assimilation, becomes obsolete when the ethnic subject agrees to become an American; but as long as the caricaturist's "bold drawn image" serves to cast the shadows of ethnic origin in exaggerated contours against the background, ethnic identity persists in dwarfing the immigrant's incipient "Americanism." The image underwrites a melting-pot ideology, inviting the Jew, the Italian, the Irishman, and other "alien types" to pursue an American dream of self-creation, even as it confounds the idea of assimilation by making ethnic identity inescapable.

The paradox of *Puck's* immigrant xenophobes animates the graphic discourse of American ethnic caricature, and the same "double-strategy" lies behind much of the ambivalent social work of American literary realism. In fact, *Puck's* circular critique of nativist anxieties, which might also be read as an expression of nativist anxieties, anticipates Henry James's representation of himself as the "perpetually provisional" analyst of *The American Scene,* a hybrid figure who is neither "as fresh as an inquiring stranger" nor "as acute as an initiated native."[7] Mark Twain generates the same tension with his oxymoronic conception of "the genuine nigger show," a formulation that pairs authenticity and imitation in another self-consciously dialectical arrangement.[8] Minstrelsy's performative caricatures constituted Twain's favorite enactment of American identity because, like James, he understood the self as neither singular nor multiple, neither entirely original nor merely imitative. As the conceptual embodiments of this paradox of identity, ethnic caricatures such as Twain's John Chinaman and Edith Wharton's incorrigible Simon Rosedale mobilize realism's most vexing questions about the origins of "character" and the nature of human identity.

It is tempting to imagine that Wharton lifted Simon Rosedale, "a plump rosy man of the blond Jewish type," directly from the illustrated pages of *Life,* much as Twain discovered Jim's graphic image through an informal survey of the comic papers (35).[9] Indeed, Carrie Fisher entertains her friends at Rosedale's expense by delivering a one-liner that might easily have accompanied one of *Life's* standard images of the obsessively materialist Jew, who is incapable of conceiving of human relations in anything but financial terms. Mimicking Rosedale's attempt to praise Lily's extraordinary demonstration at the *tableaux vivants,* she parrots the Jew's remark: " 'My God, Mrs.

Fisher, if I could get Paul Morpeth to paint her like that, the picture'd appreciate a hundred percent in ten years'" (159). The illustrated papers of the period abounded in close variants of this joke,
locating the Jew's irrepressible profit motive at the core of his identity (figure 4.6).[10] Other characters in the scene make similar obser-
vations about Lily's sexualized performance in the Bry's conservatory,
Jack Stepney going so far as to compare her to an artifact "at auc-
tion," but Rosedale's comment is unique for its candid expression of
self-interest in Lily's value as an object (158). His eagerness to complete her reification is an unnecessary reminder of why, according to
Stepney, "we don't marry Rosedale."

Virtually every mention of Rosedale in the novel includes such a
reminder, emphasizing that regardless of the progress he has made
toward social recognition, the Jew remains unalterably true to type.
Stepney's efforts to "disguise" Rosedale as a social novelty worthy of
attention in Lily's exclusive set fail, just as Kemble's coons fail at
racial impersonation and uplift, when Judy Trenor identifies him as
"the same little Jew who had been served up and rejected at the
social board a dozen times within her memory" (37). This image of
the diminutive racial epitome, the "Jew as a Jew," as *Puck* might put
it, haunts Rosedale like the shadow of his ethnic origin, revealing his
every act and intuition as manifestations of an irrepressible race
instinct. Lily is aware that Rosedale's affection for her is governed
by "his race's accuracy in the appraisal of values," and she understands that he gravitates toward her in response to "that mixture of
artistic sensibility and business astuteness which characterizes his

FIGURE 4.6. *Life* 29
(April 1897): 278.

race" (36). Rosedale's most complex emotions, such as his reaction to the "charming gesture" with which Lily forestalls his proposal of marriage, are not his own but are immediately traceable to "the tradition of his blood to accept what was conceded" (176). His effort to personalize his identity through the purchase of a fashionable home is similarly confounded by disapproving references to "the little Jew who has bought the Greiner house" (135). Whereas Judy Trenor labors within the novel to block the ethnic pariah's advance "beyond the outer limbo of the Van Osburgh crushes," Wharton seems equally determined at the narrative level to present Rosedale as the embodiment of an inflexible racial principle (37).

Yet if Wharton appears to conspire with the novel's social managers, taking comfort in Rosedale's inability to disguise his ethnic identity, she also exposes the arbitrary nature of social structures that delay his acceptance by the novel's privileged class. As David Herman has explained, Rosedale is less an outsider than he is made to feel, for his ethnicity merely "expresses the innermost essence" of the cultural elite, revealing "a generalized orientation toward buying and selling" as the "coherent theory of their unreflective praxis."[11] Seeking to disentangle this paradox, Jennie Kassanoff has theorized that race functions in the novel as "an all-purpose ideological epoxy," neutralizing the "amorphous possibilities of class and gender" by establishing "a seemingly inviolate teleology of blood."[12] Racial identity, in other words, provides a unique point of certainty in a social world otherwise given over entirely to the blurry values of materialism, and Rosedale's insistent "blood" thus marks one boundary over which Lily really does have control.

Ethnic caricature might seem to be the representational expression of this "teleology of blood," but Kassanoff overstates Wharton's interest in providing a genetic remedy for the novel's social chaos. In fact, race proves a strangely unstable epoxy in *The House of Mirth*, for Rosedale's insistent ethnic identity merely delays his steady and inevitable ascent of the novel's social and racial ladder. By the time Lily belatedly accepts his proposal of marriage, the process of social miscegenation is already well under way, for Rosedale's name has at last acquired "an enviable prominence" on the municipal committees and charitable boards that used to reject him as a matter of course (228). His cultivation of "just the right note of disdain" for the Van Osburgh crushes has secured him a place at the Trenor dinner table, and his financial dealings have placed "Wall Street under obligations that only Fifth Avenue could repay" (228). For all Wharton's apparent desire to draw a line in the sand, an ethnically specific line that might define the limit of Lily's degradation, she is at least equally interested in demonstrating that the social currency of Fifth Avenue is legal tender on Wall Street, and vice versa. Money, not blood, determines the structure of high society, which constantly adjusts to the whims of the marketplace, making room for those who can pay.

One way to account for "the slow unalterable persistency" with which Rosedale passes through the novel's finely delineated "stages" of social refinement would be to suggest that caricature simply fails as a technique for his containment (228). Yet although he literally "expand[s]" in the course of his ascent, exchanging his diminutive moniker—"the little Jew"—for something resembling a public personality, Rosedale never ceases to function explicitly as a racial representative, and in fact his social and financial successes are directly related to the "race instinct" that persists in guiding his interests in love and in business (228). Indeed, the same qualities that brand him as an outsider, such as the thick Jewish skin that "fitted him to suffer rebuffs and put up with delays," prepare Rosedale to deal successfully with the arduous process of social assimilation (127). Similarly, his aptitude for subtle calculation, an insidious trait of the generic cartoon representation, allows Rosedale to appreciate "his unusual opportunity to shine" amidst "the general dullness of the season," advancing his social interests like a stock broker who senses a fruitful buying opportunity (127). The valuable "tips" that function as a legitimate form of currency in Lily's social world belong exclusively to Rosedale because his race instinct is ironically a source of private knowledge, a kind of privileged insight into material affairs that translates directly into social prestige. Carrie Fisher orchestrates the Jew's early conquests on the social stage, but it is again "his race's accuracy in the appraisal of values" that leads Rosedale to desire the "more individual environment" that only Lily can provide (127). No one else in the novel, least of all Selden, finally knows how to measure Lily's worth as the sort of object that appreciates in value, and Rosedale knows this because he remains, for all the prominence his name has achieved, a version of the nameless "little Jew" who speculates on the value of her company in the novel's opening scenes. Indeed, the darling of Wall Street, the epitome of the self-made man, achieves an aura of "personality" by virtue of his conformity to a seemingly inflexible racial type. Rosedale's very name betokens the paradox of his identity, the affectionately abbreviated "Sim" affirming his acceptance within the novel's exclusive inner circle, even as it connotes inauthenticity ("simulation") and cheap reproducibility ("simulacrum").

Rosedale's fungible identity—his conflicted role as self-made man and ethnic representative—resonates with *Puck's* incoherent praise for the "remarkable and admirable qualities" of the "children of Israel," but Wharton's ambivalence runs deeper. Like James, who admires "the intensity of the Jewish aspect," Wharton relishes the ethnic alien's glaring otherness, which is both a threat to be contained and a source of critical power to be accessed.[13] In James's equally problematic image of Jewish New York, the Jew's potency lies in his precariously suspended condition as a citizen/outsider, a condition that unmistakably mirrors the analyst's own cultural status as a "restored absentee." The figure appeals to James as a special vehicle for analysis of the American scene, because the Jew's cosmopolitan identity, his complex relation to "America," defies simple constructions of a homogeneous national character. For Wharton, too, the Jew's scandalously "overdeveloped proboscis" functions as shorthand notation for a special brand of critique, one that demystifies the "idols" of social privilege, even as it further delineates the contours of class and ethnic identity. To be sure, Wharton betrays little affection for her "plump rosy" Jew, but her sensibility as a writer is closely aligned with the paradoxical critique that Rosedale's character sets in motion. The Jew remains a Jew in *The House of Mirth,* but Rosedale's aggressive typification also exposes the mystique of class privilege, betraying the material underpinnings of the social hierarchy through which the simply "impossible" Jew makes every acquisition possible (37). For Wharton, as for James, the irreducible duality of the caricatured ethnic subject offers a template for the ambivalent critical work of realism.

As a loosely knit group, the American realists were heavily invested in the "perpetually provisional" status afforded this curious figure, the social alien whose exaggerated characterization blends xenophobic anxiety with immanent critique. Howells, Twain, James, and many of their contemporaries were interested in affirming the existence of a stable social reality, one grounded in nature and buttressed by a liberal conception of autonomous selfhood, and their sometimes brutal representations of ethnic subjects served this essentially conservative project by marking off the boundaries of a privileged ethnic identity. But the same writers were profoundly suspicious of the ideological drift of late nineteenth-century capitalism, and their distorted ethnic *arrivistes* often participated in a devastating analysis of the structures of American privilege. Racial caricature constituted the realist writer's most effective means of suspending these dual imperatives in a form of critique that manages to be wildly inconsistent without lapsing into mere contradiction.

This critique often takes place at the dramatic margins of the realist novel, where a character like Basil March momentarily becomes aware of the nether world existing just beyond the reach of his carefully managed field of vision. But the margins have been folded inward in *The House of Mirth,* where the duplicitous logic of ethnic caricature operates as a paradigm for understanding identity itself, including that of the period's most charismatic racial epitome, Lily Bart. Observing the way Lily's racialized outline stands "relieved against the dull tints of the crowd" at the beginning of the novel, Lawrence Selden wonders if her beauty is the expression of some utterly unique, private essence of personality, or if her "conspicuous" image amounts to nothing more than a representation of "the civilization which had produced her" (26, 29). This "confused sense" of Lily's substance haunts Selden throughout the novel, piquing his interest in her social career, even as it cripples his romantic designs (27). At the heart of his dilemma is a question about ethnic origins: is Miss Bart the member of a more "specialized" race, as Selden occasionally suspects, or is her beauty merely the expression of a cultural ideal, "as though a fine glaze of beauty and fastidiousness had been applied to applied to vulgar clay" (27)? Although keenly aware that "the qualities distinguishing her from the herd of her sex were chiefly external," Selden theorizes that "a course texture will not take a high finish," and he thus provisionally concludes that the sources of Lily's peculiar charm must lie within (27). The question of her ethnic origin persists, however, and Selden wavers uncertainly between a romantic assumption that Lily's beauty is perfectly original and a lurking suspicion that her image is nothing more than an expensive product of convention.

To share Selden's uncertainty is to understand Lily as an ethnic caricature. Like Rosedale, who generates a semblance a "personality" by acting on his race instincts, Lily achieves an air of detachment from the glittering social world—an air of originality and independence—at precisely those moments when she most fully embodies its ethnic ideal. Her performance as "Mrs. Lloyd" at the *tableaux vivants* is only one example of her unrivaled gift for infusing lifeless social rituals with the warm breath of an inimitable personality. As one of the period's most compelling and problematic ethnic caricatures, she blends an exaggerated conformity to "type" with an intoxicating sense of originality, producing in admirers such as Selden a version of the ambivalence that powers the engine of ethnic misrepresentation from the pages of *Puck* to those of *The House of Mirth*.

Selden wishes to see his way out of this ambivalence when he reflects on Lily's racial exceptionality, noting the distance that separates her face and figure from those of "sallow-faced girls in preposterous hats, and flat-chested women struggling with paper bundles and palm-leaf fans" (27). Observing such discrepancies of skin color and body shape, he wonders if Lily's finely articulated, immobile white figure belongs "to the same race," a speculation that recurs even among more refined company, as when he admires "the way in which she detached herself, by a hundred undefinable shades, from the persons who most abounded in her own style" (27, 206). Interpreting Lily's exquisite charm as evidence of a unique ethnic disposition, he discounts the significance of her Anglo-Dutch genealogy, preferring to notice "the differences" that emerge "with special poignancy" when Lily moves among her socially prestigious friends and relatives (207).

Selden is not the only character who regards Lily as a racial anomaly. In fact, she endorses this reading of herself as an exquisite freak of nature and works hard to make "her grace, her quickness, her social felicities" appear like the natural expressions of a unique ethnicity (206). Elaborating on Selden's suspicion that she belongs to a separate race, Lily offers a more precise account of her own ethnic constitution when she explains that people like Percy Gryce and Gwen Van Osburgh, regular members of her social set, "wouldn't look at each other, they never do. Each of them wants a creature of a different race, of Jack's race and mine, with all sorts of intuitions, sensations, and perceptions they don't even guess the existence of" (64).

Gryce is neither Jewish nor does he belong to the world of anonymous labor, where flat-chested women struggle with paper bundles, and yet he fails to qualify as a member of Lily's "race" because he lacks an aura of originality, an aura that emanates from the apparent independence with which Lily conforms to the most rigid social conventions. Unlike Rosedale, whose affectations of social distinction remain laughably transparent, Gryce knows the forms and codes that regulate elite social life, and he practices them with uncritical enthusiasm. But the formal conventions that delineate his class identity do not express Gryce's "personality," which remains hopelessly sheltered from view. Thus despite his class status, he impresses Lily as a kind of imitation, a racial imposter whose unfitness to perform the graces of social life is as marked as that of his Jewish rival. The narrator observes that "Gryce was handsome in a didactic way—he looked like a clever pupil's drawing from a plaster cast—while Gwen's countenance had no more modeling than a face painted on a toy balloon" (64).

Although they enjoy uncontested prestige among the novel's social elite, Percy Gryce and Gwen Van Osburgh are racial inferiors in that they appear like cheap reproductions of some remote original. As the amateurish copy of a copy, Gryce is oddly a caricature of himself, and the glaring discrepancy between his finished image and the racial principle to which it refers disqualifies him, much as it disqualifies the relentlessly imitative Jew, as a desirable suitor for Lily's hand in marriage. Gwen Van Osburgh's racial inferiority is equally measurable in terms of the distance that separates her formless countenance from an origin. As Lily watches Gwen and Jack Stepney perform the rituals of courtship at Bellomont, she is struck with "a certain annoyance in contemplating what seemed to her a caricature of her own situation" (63). Only Selden impresses Lily as "belonging to a more specialized race" by virtue of the "keenly-modelled dark features" that give his face an appearance of originality "in a land of amorphous types" (79).

The "more specialized race" to which Lily and Selden ostensibly belong is not, of course, a "race" in the usual sense, for one qualifies for membership only by generating an impression of perfect racelessness, of perfect independence from the generic features of any "type." Selden's "republic of the spirit," which he calls "a country one has to find the way to one's self," is the spiritual homeland of this paradoxical "race" of human originals, whose members enjoy "personal freedom . . . from all the material accidents" (80–81). Lily has the shrewdness to object that the *jeune fille a marier,* whose opportunities for self-expression are so narrowly prescribed by convention, has no place in such a utopian landscape (82). Yet as Selden observes with confusion throughout the novel, her most contrived performances produce a thrilling sense of authenticity, such that the most conventional pieties of the drawing room appear in Lily like "the overflow of a bounteous nature" (206). Not even Bertha Dorset, Lily's principal rival, belongs to her "race," for Bertha's social histrionics impress Selden as "too free, too fluent, for perfect naturalness," and "perfect naturalness" in the performance of rigid social conventionalities is the essence of Lily's exclusive racial identity (207).

Lily's ability to mystify prestige produces an intriguing detour in the usual logic of ethnic caricature. Much as Rosedale serves throughout the novel as a representative of his race, so is the lily-white Miss Bart an unmistakable racial epitome, "the fine flower" of Anglo-Dutch womanhood, whose exaggerated "smoothness" and "purity of tint" denote a specific genealogy (207, 26). But if Rosedale wears his thick Jewish skin like a visible badge of identity, Lily's status as "the complete expression of the state she aspired to" depends on her ability to conceal ethnic identifiers in order to seem perfectly original (207). The race she epitomizes, in other words, understands itself as raceless, and Lily qualifies as its representative only to the extent that she successfully perpetuates this illusion in the realm of social convention.

The same paradox animates representations of the American woman of fashion in humor magazines of the period. Dehumanizing images of the Jew, the Irishman, and the African American certainly produced the era's most arresting graphic commentary on American ethnic identity, but no cultural "type" received more attention from caricaturists than the white woman of fashion, whose aristocratic pretensions were often ridiculed and subtly legitimized within the space of a single image. Among the humor magazines, *Life* was particularly vigorous in portraying American women as slaves to fashion, dreamy beauties who participate enthusiastically in their own reification. An 1897 image of an elegant woman, whose jewelry, hair, and facial features are represented by dollar signs, employs a motif usually reserved for the Jew in American caricature, but which here conveys the substance of Thorstein Veblen's popular thesis that the American woman of leisure is nothing more than an objectified display of her husband's wealth (figure 4.7).[14]

Life's disdain for feminine posturing—coupled with the magazine's pronounced opposition to women's suffrage—produced an aggressively condescending graphic discourse, but the white woman of fashion is remarkable among the period's ethnic types for the fact that she possesses no physiologically distinguishing features. Her graphic signature, equivalent to the Jew's nose or the Irishman's distended jaw, is usually an elaborate hat, an absurdly ornamental wig, or some other explicitly superficial object of her depraved material appetites (figure 4.8). Ethnic caricature, of course, typically reduces its subject to some inflexible attribute of type, fixing the margins of

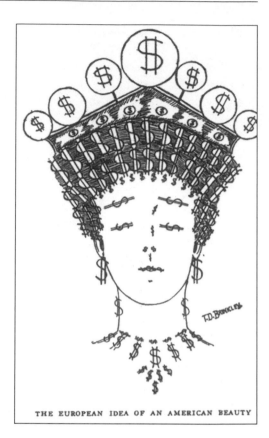

THE EUROPEAN IDEA OF AN AMERICAN BEAUTY

FIGURE 4.7. T. D. Brinkley,
Life 55 (April 1910): 648.

ethnic identity by exaggerating physiognomic and cultural indicators of origin. A subversive potential emerges when those indicators are so grossly distorted as to become arbitrary symbolic clichés, which serve to disguise ethnic identity as effectively as they purport to reveal it. Exaggerated images of the American woman of fashion operate differently, for her distinguishing characteristic is an arbitrary disguise that ineffectively conceals a normative ideal of feminine beauty. The fashionable American woman is a deplorably predictable type, in other words, only until the caricatured image reveals her to be what she has been all along: a typeless original. Whereas caricatures of the period generally serve to contain the uppity "coon" or the socially ambitious Jew by emphasizing his inevitable conformity to type, the American woman of fashion is an original masquerading as a type. In her case, the caricatured image exaggerates only what is extraneous to identity, not what is putatively essential, revealing the elaborately decorated female subject as, at bottom, an ethnic original who enjoys natural prestige and an authentic aristocratic bearing.

This modified logic of ethnic caricature operates explicitly in *Life*'s cover for the 1910 "Fashion Number," which featured two images of "The Milkmaid," one as she appears in reality, the other as she is represented on stage (figure 4.9). This stark comparison underscores an assumption that informs virtually every caricature of the

FIGURE 4.8. "Easter Thoughts," *Life*, date unknown.

FIGURE 4.9. "The Milkmaid," *Life* 55 (April 1910): cover.

society girl during the period, the assumption that behind the distorting guise of high fashion lies "the real thing," the authentic
American woman, impervious to the habit of emulation, capable of
hard work, naturally modest, and irresistibly beautiful. Her warm
and sober stare distinguishes her from any conceivable type; indeed,
unlike her stage counterpart, whose upturned nose mimics the
frozen expressions of "the golden mien," she is the type of typeless-
ness, the ethnic original to which every mere copy inadequately
refers. Her presence is generally hidden beneath the absurdly extra-

SOCIETY (ISLAND) NOTE
" THE GROOM WORE THE CONVENTIONAL
BLACK."

FIGURE 4.10. "Society (Island) Note,"
Life 55 (April 1910): 690.

neous ornaments and accessories with which the society woman
masks her true identity, but she is always implicitly there as a rebuke
to what *Life* deemed the "foolish frumpery of fashion."[15]

Life's "Society (Island) Note" hints at the different logic at work
when "coon" symbolism enters into the same form of critique (figure
4.10). Like "The Milkmaid," this image pokes fun at the hollow for-
malism of social rituals by demonstrating that "conventional black"
takes on an entirely new meaning in the tropics. Wearing only a
loincloth and a few primitive ornaments, the savage groom offers a
glimpse of what "conventional black" usually conceals—namely, the
reality of the body—much as the country milkmaid reveals the feminine essence behind the merely symbolic costume worn by her stage
counterpart. Both illustrations betray the corrupt vocabulary of high

fashion with a comic gesture toward the authentic inner core of the caricatured image. But the resemblance ends here, for the "Society (Island) Note" offers no refuge from the debasement of type. Conventional formal attire is a false signifier of social prestige, the image suggests, yet the couple's bulbous lips confirm that the ethnic figures who allow us to see through the pretense of formal clothing are themselves the products of convention. The preacher's minstrel top hat and painted smile similarly imply that two meanings of "conventional black" are at play in the illustration, and that they are equally ridiculous. Unlike "The Milkmaid," which traces a cultural type to its unacculturated origin beyond ethnicity, the "Society (Island) Note" suggests that, for the "coon," there is no end to emulation and no alternative to type.

Edith Wharton would have enjoyed this joke. Selden, to be sure, reads Lily's character according to the racial mythology at work in "The Milkmaid," and his effort to "disengage" the real Lily from the figure produced by convention intends to impose that illustration's idealistic logic on her story. For Wharton, on the other hand, such disengagement from the codes and rituals of cultural life comes at a horrible sacrifice to identity. As the social prominence of dubious financiers like Sim Rosedale and Julius Beaufort in *The Age of Innocence* confirms, ethnic boundaries are transgressable in Wharton's fictional world, where the obstacles to social mobility are always vulnerable to readjustment. These social climbers routinely change tribes, and yet no character in Wharton's fiction enjoys the freedom to opt out of tribal life itself. Wharton's curious satires hinge on this paradox: although deeply committed to exposing the arbitrary nature of social practices that inhibit human freedom, she is as deeply suspicious of any human practice that pretends to stand outside of culture. Contrary to Selden's idealism, which finds powerful expression in the era's exaggerated representation of the white woman of fashion, Wharton's art finally coincides more fully with the comic sensibility of the "Society (Island) Note," for she cannot imagine a point of conscious origin prior to acculturation, any more than she can conceive of a social space beyond the reach of convention.

This is a cumbersome way of making a point already advanced by some of Wharton's best critics. In a brilliant essay entitled "Disowning 'Personality': Privacy and Subjectivity in *The House of Mirth*," William Moddelmog explores the meaning of these contentious terms in turn-of-the-century legal discourse, arguing that Wharton conceives of the self "relationally," not as a unitary or discrete psychological entity.[16] Pamela Knights makes a closely related point by reading Wharton through the lens of early twentieth-century sociology, which challenged the model of autonomous selfhood by theorizing that "personality develops within discourse."[17] Amy Kaplan's analysis of the writer's professional identity similarly concludes that, for Wharton, "personality" originates in a complicated synthesis of private and public forces, neither of which are sufficient in themselves to sustain a viable sense of identity.[18] These critics concur that Wharton understands the self as a paradox, a version of ethnic caricature's endless interplay of authenticity and imitation, which manifests itself in such unpredictable characters as Undine Spragg, who is described as "fiercely independent and yet passionately imitative."[19] Lily Bart similarly blends an instinct for social conformity with an unyielding independent streak, a combination that, in her finest moments, makes craven imitation appear like the expression of a "specialized" ethnic disposition.

Selden's ambivalence toward Lily stems from his mistrust of this fundamental dialectic. Although he enjoys the touch of "naturalness" she bring to the stiff formalities of the drawing room, Selden practices a crude and self-serving Emersonianism that makes a fetish of "personal freedom," and thus he fantasizes recklessly about removing Lily—"the real Lily"—from the network of conventions that constitute her identity (81). "*That is how she looks when she is alone!*" he imagines with characteristic zeal as he encounters Lily in the gardens at Bellomont, a conjecture that traces her ineffable appeal to a private source somewhere beyond the realm of mere social display (82; emphasis in original). From their first unconventional meeting in his apartment, detachment from the "material accidents" of social life—"from money, from poverty, from ease and anxiety"—has been the precondition of their intimacy, for Selden's faith assumes the existence of a private, "inviolate self," a psychological entity that preexists the social marketplace and that might be capable, under the right circumstances, of retreat to some "republic of the spirit" (81).[20] His romantic emotions are governed by this faith in "privacy" as a natural condition, rather than, as Lily understands it, a luxury available only to those who can afford it. In constantly striving to imagine Lily apart from her surroundings, he intends to reclaim "the real Lily," the racially specialized, organic original, who "stands apart" from the amorphous crowd, whether the crowd gathers at Grand Central or at Newport.

But "the real Lily" has more in common with Mark Twain's oxy-

moronic "real coons" than Selden is capable of understanding, and
indeed ethnic caricature functions throughout the novel as a rebuke
to Selden's naive romanticism. Although Selden labors unsuccess-
fully to extricate Lily's private image from the social trappings "that
cheapened and vulgarized it," Wharton subtly reveals the private
Lily as herself the product of an exaggerated ethnic performance. Although she cultivates a romance of self-identity in her admirers,
brandishing a personal seal with the legend "Beyond" etched in styl-
ish lettering, Lily remains attuned to the hypocrisy of Selden's tran-
scendental view of the self, and she continually and self-consciously
produces herself as the embodiment a racial concept whose essence is
irreproducibility. In fact, her knack for exaggerated ethnic self-representation is worthy of comparison with that of the dance phenomenon Juba, who became the most famous African-American performer of the 1840s by doing imitations of white dancers imitating
him, and whose act concluded with an authentic "imitation of himself."[21] As in the crude comedy of the "Society (Island) Note," ethnic self-parody here explodes the illusion of a unitary subject, insisting that "authentic" identity always entails an element of racialized
performance. Lily cannot simply "be herself," as Selden desires, for
"the real Lily"—like the real Sim Rosedale or "The Two Real
Coons"—is a complicated blend of private essences and cultural
clichés, a dynamic Lily herself begins to appreciate late in the novel
when she learns to regard herself as "a flamboyant copy" of her former self, "a caricature approximating the real thing as the 'society
play' approximates the manners of the drawing-room" (222).

Wharton explores the rich comedy implied by this insight—the
notion that one is always somehow a caricature of oneself—in the
novel's central episode, the *tableaux vivants,* where the women of
Lily's set vie for male attention by exhibiting themselves in a series of
explicitly racialized performances. Like the living caricatures of
Twain's "genuine minstrel show," the performers in Paul Morpeth's
tableaux vivants entertain their audience by blurring the line between type and individual, subduing the "fugitive curves of living
flesh" to "plastic harmony without losing the charm of life" (138).
Under Morpeth's artistic direction, the ladies have been "cleverly fitted with characters suited to their types," so that the dark-skinned
Carry Fisher makes a "typical Goya," whereas Mrs. Van Alstyne,
"who showed the frailer Dutch type, with high blue-veined forehead
and pale eyes and lashes," effectively presents a "characteristic
Vandyck" (138). Each artfully crafted exhibit of feminine beauty suc-

ceeds by subordinating the individual features of the performer to some ethnic or cultural principle. Like Percy Gryce's generic countenance, the living images that follow one another across the Bry conservatory stage "with the rhythmic march of some splendid frieze" are copies of copies, performative ethnic caricatures that depend for their effect on "the exaggerated glow" of dark eyes, or the "provocation of [a] frankly painted smile" (138).

Amidst this march of plastic cultural types, Lily's performance is apparently unique. "[S]o skillfully had the personality of the actors been subdued to the scenes they figured in," according to the narrator, "that even the least imaginative of the audience must have felt a thrill of contrast when the curtain suddenly parted on a picture that was simply and undisguisedly the portrait of Miss Bart" (138). With no sacrifice to her own originality, Lily produces a stunning impression of Joshua Reynolds's "Mrs. Lloyd," inverting the process of plastic representation by stepping "not out of, but into, Reynolds's canvas, banishing his dead beauty by her living grace" (138). Whereas the individual characteristics of her fellow performers are absorbed in the representation of various cultural types, Lily dawns on the stage "with no mistaking the predominance of personality," her indomitable originality causing her to appear more like the model for Reynolds's canvas than like a twice-removed interpretation (138). Having resisted a momentary impulse to portray Tiepolo's exotic Cleopatra, Lily "had shown her artistic intelligence in selecting a type so like her own that she could embody the person represented without ceasing to be herself" (139). Indeed, her "dryad-like curves" so thoroughly defy typification that Selden, "for the first time . . . seemed to see before him the real Lily Bart, divested of the trivialities of her little world" (139).

Selden's idealism reaches a laughable pitch in this hollow tribute, which utterly misreads Lily's performance as an affirmation of autonomous selfhood. Instead of divesting her image from "all that cheapened and vulgarized it," Lily's demonstration places her beauty in the service of the Wellington Brys, whose crass social ambitions lie squarely behind the evening's elaborate entertainment. Moreover, Lily's performance is no less the enactment of an ethnic principle than is Carrie Fisher's dark-skinned Goya, with the important difference that the "type" Lily epitomizes—what might be called the type of self-effacing Anglo-Saxon womanhood—presents itself as a raceless ideal. As the premier academic portraitist of eighteenth-century England, president of the Royal Academy since its founding in 1768,

Sir Joshua Reynolds would have been well known among Lily's set for the ardent nationalism of his famous *Discourses,* which articulated "the Englishness of English art" for generations of British and American successors.[22] Given Lily's situation as a single girl with uncertain marriage prospects, her choice of "Mrs. Lloyd," a painting that celebrates the steadfastness of the British character by representing a young matron in the act of etching her husband's name on a tree, suggests multiple ironies, all of which disappear in Selden's twisted interpretation of the performance as an expression of Lily's "real self." In fact, Lily never appears more "real," more individual and authentic, than when she presents herself as the embodiment of a cultural idea, which is to say that the "real Lily" is always a caricature, a "flamboyant copy" of some putative ethnic original.

Among her variously unsavory suitors, Rosedale alone understands that Lily's identity is negotiated at the intersection of public and private worlds, where the self is never entirely identical with itself, but is constantly engaged in acts of self-representation and self-parody. Rather than hope to disengage Lily's image from the "material accidents" of social life, he proposes to place a crown on her head. Some women look "buried under their jewelry," he explains. "What I want is a woman who will hold her head higher the more diamonds I put on it. And when I looked at you the other night at the Brys,' in that plain white dress, looking as if you had a crown on, I said to myself: 'By gad, if she had one she'd wear it as if it grew on her'" (175).

Having witnessed the same performance that inspires Selden's paean to individual freedom, Rosedale offers a significantly different account of "the real Lily." Noting that the personalities of her fellow performers are "subdued" through conformity to type, like the personalities of women who appear "buried under their jewelry," he regards Lily's *tableau* as exceptional, not for her rejection of "the trivialities of her little world," but for her ability to make them seem like a birthright. He acknowledges the histrionic element in this ritual of self-representation when he comments that Lily would wear her crown "as if" it grew on her head, replacing Selden's naive organicism with a more ironic and sincere appreciation for her part as an actress in a social play. Hoping to cast Lily as the star in his own drama of ethnic uplift and transformation, Rosedale offers neither to bury nor to liberate her, but rather invites Lily to assume a firmer hold on the representative status she already enjoys, if only provisionally, as the "fine flower" of Anglo-Dutch New York. Ironically—

even perversely—it is Lily's commitment to "privacy," not her own but Selden's, that prevents this arrangement.

Perhaps it is Rosedale's position at the margins of the social world, himself an ethnic caricature of the most conventional sort, that allows him to recognize Lily Bart's uniqueness as inseparable from her typicality. Armed with "his race's accuracy in the appraisal of values," he might agree that Lily is the era's most intriguing carica-ture of the white woman of fashion, in part because Wharton does not accept the popular culture's self-understanding of white privilege as scripted in nature. Her critique draws on the more cynical re-sources of "coon" comedy and anti-Semitic caricature to suggest, with *Life*'s "Society (Island) Note," that there is no end to emulation and no refuge from the types of human identity.

5

The "Curious Realism" of Charles W. Chesnutt

As an "American of acknowledged African descent," according to his own description, Charles Chesnutt had more to lose and less to gain from the practice of ethnic caricature than any of the other writers considered in these pages.[1] The "bold drawn image" of ethnic alienism may have performed an imperfect defensive function for writers who shared Henry James's sense of "dispossession," but Chesnutt can only have experienced the proliferation of "coon" humor at the close of the nineteenth century as a personal humiliation.[2] Indeed, his creative ambitions took shape against the crude assumption embedded in Ernest Hogan's unforgettable refrain, "all coons look alike to me," words that resounded throughout the era, to Chesnutt's dismay, like a popular mantra.[3] Nevertheless, of all the writers discussed in this book, only Chesnutt received his literary training in the heterogeneous pages of *Puck,* and no writer ultimately learned to command the reductive logic of ethnic caricature with more purpose.

The appearance of "The Goophered Grapevine" in the August 1887 issue of the *Atlantic Monthly* typically marks the starting point for scholarly discussion of Chesnutt's career, but he had reached a national audience already during the spring of that year with the publication of his first *Puck* sketch, "Appreciation."[4] Over the next two years, he composed short comic pieces for *Tid-Bits, Family Fiction, Household Realm,* and other magazines, including a total of nine sketches for *Puck.* When they have bothered to mention this minor body of work at all, Chesnutt's critics have generally accepted William Andrews's reasonable opinion that the early sketches were

no more than formulaic "hackwork," and yet *Puck* ironically provided a fruitful setting for Chesnutt's literary apprenticeship.[5] The
magazine's no-holds-barred approach to ethnic humor was surely
formulaic, but the sheer abundance of exaggerated ethnic signifiers
within its pages produced an almost chaotic impression of racial mobility, an impression oddly compatible with Chesnutt's conception
of human identity.

At the heart of this conception lay the belief that racial "integrity"—a buzzword of late nineteenth-century social theory—is "a
modern invention of the white people to perpetuate the color line."[6]
Chesnutt considered the cultural and physical characteristics that ostensibly differentiate the "races" of mankind to be "superficial and
inconstant," and he theorized that when the members of different
ethnic groups mingle socially, amalgamation is the inevitable and biologically desirable consequence.[7] The only race with a legitimate
basis in scientific fact, in his view, is the human race, which will im-
prove as a species though the "greater efficiency" of an inclusive organization of humanity.[8]

Chesnutt articulated these unfashionable beliefs with unflinching candor for nearly fifty years, from his earliest polemical essays
of the 1880s, until shortly before his death in 1932. In the landmark
1889 essay "What Is a White Man?," he attacked "whiteness" as
a pernicious legal fiction, maintaining that although "the line which
separates the races" in the United States has been "practically ob-
literated," its potent legacy continues to inform a corrupt legal discourse that embraces the leading assumptions of nineteenth-century
pseudoscience.[9] According to accepted usage, he argued, the term
"Anglo-Saxon" refers incoherently to groups with widely divergent
physical and cultural characteristics, including Teutons, Gauls, Slavs,
and Jews, whereas Americans who possess even imperceptible traces
of African ancestry are deemed members of a discrete racial category.
Legal distinctions based on such specious reasoning, according to
Chesnutt, ignore the findings of contemporary anthropology in
order to perpetuate an anachronistic fantasy of white mastery.

The point is reiterated even more emphatically in Chesnutt's series of three essays contributed to the Boston *Evening Transcript* in
1900, collectively entitled "The Future American." In the first installment, "What the Race Is Likely to Become in the Process of
Time," he declares that "[a]ny dream of a pure white race, of the
Anglo-Saxon type, for the United States, may as well be abandoned
as impossible," for "conditions of trade and ease of travel are likely to

gradually assimilate to one type" the people who inhabit "the northern hemisphere of the western continent."[10] This future American
ethnic type "will be formed of a mingling, in a yet to be ascertained
proportion," of North America's three numerically significant populations, indigenous peoples, former slaves of African origin, and European immigrants (123). Future Americans will call themselves
white, Chesnutt concedes, as long as it is in their political and economic interest to do so, but prophesies about absolute hegemony in
the Western hemisphere by a biologically identifiable white population are based on "hoary anthropological fallacies" that ignore "the
facts of human nature and human history" (123). In truth, "there are
no natural obstacles to such an amalgamation," and "the formation
of a uniform type out of our present racial elements will take place
within a measurably near period" (125).

Such opinions found few champions in late nineteenth-century
America, even among those who professed to hold liberal views on
what was pejoratively called "the Negro question," and yet Chesnutt's radical social vision was strangely at home within the pages of
Puck. This is not to suggest that the paper's editorial wing shared his
reading of "human nature and human history," for it certainly did
not. Yet *Puck*'s relentless insensitivity toward every imaginable "racial
element" produced a striking, if inadvertent, egalitarianism. This
was partly a result of the paper's layout, which sought to maximize
the reader's entertainment by cluttering the page with often incoherent juxtapositions of ethnic imagery. Crowding the two modest
columns of Chesnutt's sketch "How a Good Man Went Wrong," for
example, are an illustration of a "coon" preacher, Rev. Sim Goose-
berry of 'Possum Bottom, West Virginia, and a cartoon featuring
two disreputable looking Irish policemen, bearing the legend "Brute
Force." Nestled directly between Chesnutt's finely printed columns,
whose margins open outward to form a textual frame, is an illustration entitled "Lavishness at Hochstein's," which satirizes the squalor
of Jewish tenement life in New York (figure 5.1). None of these images bears even a remote thematic relevance to Chesnutt's sketch
about a municipal employee mistakenly accused of stealing public
funds, unless perhaps *Puck*'s editors meant to suggest an abstract
connection between Hochstein's exaggerated parsimony and the
story's defalcation theme. In any case, the interpenetration of image
and text across the page produces the effect of an ethnic smorgas-
bord, inviting readers to engage in something like a process of free
association with ethnic clichés. The impulse behind any one of

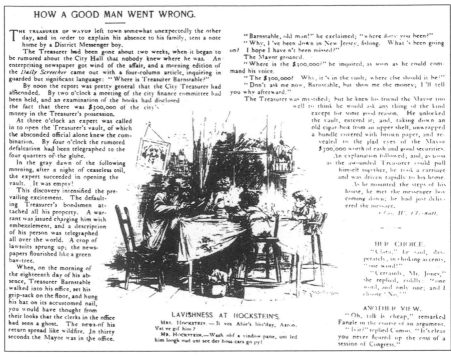

FIGURE 5.1. "Lavishness at Hockstein's," *Puck* (November 28, 1888): 214.

Puck's illustrations or anecdotes may have been straightforwardly condescending, but the intimate grouping of such heterogeneous material made the paper a unique laboratory for the blending of "our present racial elements" into unexpected new combinations.

Formatting decisions in *Puck* occasionally reflected a more coherent editorial design, as the appearance of Chesnutt's "A Roman Antique" in the July 17, 1889, issue demonstrates. This brief sketch records a conversation between two strangers, the narrator—an affluent, educated, white New Yorker—and a "white haired Negro," who seats himself beside the other on a Washington Square bench, "lifting his battered hat deferentially" as he does so. "How old are you, Uncle?" asks the younger man, to which his companion responds with a yarn about his upbringing under slavery, before "de wah broke out," when he belonged to "Mars Julius." The narrator objects to the old man's chronology, noting that this would make him only forty years old, but the storyteller explains that the war in question was "de las' wah wid Gaul," and "Mars Julius" was the

Roman general Caesar. In return for saving his master's life in "de battle ob Alesia," the old man continues, "'Mars Julius gun me a quartah, en w'en he died, he lef' directions in his will fer me ter be gradu'lly 'mancipated, so I 'ud be free w'en I wuz a hund'ed years ole. Ah, but dem wuz good ole times,' he added, with a sigh of regret. 'I's done spent de quartah Mars Julius gun me,' he remarked, giving me a sidelong look, 'en I needs ernudder fer ter git some liniment fer my rheumatiz. Is yer got any small change 'bout yo' clo's, boss?'"

The narrator inadvertently acknowledges the legitimacy of this thinly veiled plea for reparations when, "in a fit of abstraction," he hands the old man a twenty-dollar gold piece instead of a quarter. Much as Uncle Julius employs antebellum superstition to manipulate John's charitable instincts in Chesnutt's conjure stories, here the former slave asserts not only his need, but his right to material assistance by referring first to his exploitation during the "good ole times" of slavery, and then to the enduring crime of gradual emancipation.

Puck's choice of a graphic corollary, however, suggests a different reading. Unlike the seemingly random profusion of ethnic images that surrounds the text of "How a Good Man Went Wrong," E. W. Kemble's illustration of an "outraged ostrich" implies a deliberate, if puzzling, commentary on Chesnutt's sketch (figure 5.2). The black figure in Kemble's image, like Chesnutt's talkative beggar, subsists by taking from others; in this case, he actually sucks life from the ostrich's nest. Yet although in Chesnutt's account the white man plays the role of "sucker" in a con game justified by history, Kemble's pun turns the joke against itself, representing the black figure as both a beggar and a "sucker," trapped in a confrontation he neither can nor deserves to win. According to the illustration that physically bisects Chesnutt's text, the white figure has been "laying for" his black victim all along.

If he noticed at all, Chesnutt probably bristled at *Puck*'s demeaning illustration, but such unpredictable, inversive, and often incoherent juxtapositions of ethnic signifiers in image and text produced an excitingly heterogeneous reading experience. The overall tenor of *Puck*'s ethnic offerings remained unambiguously offensive, but the paper's motto—"what fools these mortals be"—called for an even-handed application of the caricaturist's technique, and in fact "the bachelor," "the society girl," and "the divorcee" were as often ridiculed in its pages as the Jew, the African American, or the Irish-

FIGURE 5.2. "There's Many a True Word Spoken in Jest,"
Puck (July 17, 1889): 351.

man. The polemical interests of a writer such as Chesnutt were sometimes muddled by such an erratic brand of comedy, but nowhere in late nineteenth-century American culture could one have found a more tangible example of the "mingling, in a yet to be ascertained proportion," of the ethnic varieties of the United States.

The unpredictability of *Puck*'s discourse on ethnic identity allowed Chesnutt to present himself in a number of guises and to approach issues of racial justice from multiple angles. In keeping with the paper's elusive racial politics, his own ethnicity remains obscure in sketches that typically employ the omniscient perspective of an unidentified gentleman writer or that of a white businessman thrust into contact with lower-class ethnic figures. As a result, the direction of Chesnutt's satire in many of the sketches would have been difficult for contemporary readers to pin down, and issues of special con-

cern to African Americans were sometimes enfolded within larger
concerns about citizenship and ethnicity. One of the most compelling sketches of this early period, "A Fatal Restriction," for example, describes the misfortunes of a German immigrant, Fritz Brodenwasser, who hangs himself by the neck with an American flag when
he learns of the Constitutional provision that "no person except a
natural born citizen, or a citizen of the United States at the time of
the adoption of the Constitution, shall be eligible to the office of
President."[11] When the narrator tries to reason with Fritz, pointing
out that the chances of becoming president are remote even for a
native-born American, the young immigrant cannot be consoled. A
suicide note declares: "Your cruel Constitution is responsible for my
untimely end. If I had been born in America, I may never have been
President; but I might have hoped. But now there is nothing left for
me but despair and death."

One imagines that a writer such as Chesnutt, who felt severely
restrained by conventions governing the representation of African-
American character, may have taken a perverse form of pleasure in
this rigid application of a different set of ethnic clichés. Brodenwasser's unyielding political idealism signals his Teutonic ethnic disposition, just as surely as the pretzel and sausage links that frame his
graphic image (figure 5.3). But the sketch does more than poke fun
at the excessive enthusiasm of the "whole-souled, full-faced German
youth," for Brodenwasser's fate is less that of the German as an ethnic type than that of any American who falls short of what Chesnutt
considered an abstractly conceived ideal of citizenship. In accordance with *Puck*'s sometimes frantic layering of ethnic signifiers, the
story evokes a crisis facing African Americans of the period, namely
the systematic erosion of protections guaranteed by the Fourteenth
and Fifteenth Amendments to the Constitution. The "fatal restriction" that drives Brodenwasser to suicide may be absurdly inconsequential, and his violent reaction may be nothing more than Chesnutt's comic rendering of a presumed idiosyncrasy of the German
type. But anyone who read newspapers regularly in 1889 knew that
African Americans were being lynched in the South for attempting
to exercise their rights as citizens to vote in public elections. For
black Americans in the age of Jim Crow, as Chesnutt was acutely
aware, constitutional limitations on citizenship were indeed matters
of life and death, and readers who found something to laugh at in
the image of Brodenwasser's body hanging from an American flag
beside an open copy of the Constitution cannot have entirely missed

FIGURE 5.3. Untitled illustration for "A Fatal Restriction," *Puck* (May 1, 1889): 166.

the parallel. The sketch is certainly crude, yet in a move that anticipates Chesnutt's finest efforts in fiction, he applies the thick brush of
ethnic caricature not merely to stigmatize the German, but to explore the psychological consequences of stigmatization upon human
beings of every racial variety. *Puck*'s gallery of ethnic misfits enabled
this basic maneuver of Chesnutt's art, for the paper taught him to
challenge the dehumanizing force of ethnic caricature in his own
writing by inhabiting, rather than resisting, the forms that threatened to limit his aspirations.

The full potential of this brand of critique is on display in a more harrowing account of ethnic suicide, "Dave's Neckliss," which appeared in the October, 1889, issue of the *Atlantic Monthly,* just five months after *Puck*'s publication of "A Fatal Restriction."[12] The story was Chesnutt's third for the *Atlantic* in a series of narrative encounters between the white northern couple, John and Annie, and their African-American coachman, Uncle Julius, a former slave and native of the couple's plantation home in postwar North Carolina. As in the earlier stories, "The Goophered Grapevine" and "Po' Sandy," Julius entertains his new employers with a yarn about antebellum days, although the absence of conjure as a narrative element in "Dave's Neckliss" reflected Chesnutt's desire to "get out of the realm of superstition [and] into the realm of feeling and passion."[13] This new emphasis produced his most elaborate meditation on the dynamics of ethnic caricature, as John's lengthy characterization of Uncle Julius in the story's opening frame begins to suggest. With his "curiously undeveloped nature," according to John, Julius was

> subject to moods which were almost childish in their variableness. It was only now and then that we were able to study, through the medium of his recollection, the simple but intensely human inner life of slavery. . . . While he mentioned with a warm appreciation the acts of kindness which those in authority had shown to him and his people, he would speak of a cruel deed, not with the indignation of one accustomed to quick feeling and spontaneous expression, but with a furtive disapproval which suggested to us a doubt in his own mind as to whether he had a right to think or to feel, and presented to us the curious psychological spectacle of a mind enslaved long after the shackles had been struck off from the limbs of its possessor. (124)

John's impression of the freedman's perpetual psychological enslavement is apparently borne out in the tale. Dave is a pious and hardworking slave, until he is punished for a theft he did not commit by having a ham shackled to his neck. This token of his reification under slavery puts an end to Dave's intellectual growth—he had become literate—and destroys his standing as an organizer of the black religious community. The ham (which, as Eric Sundquist points out, recalls the biblical Ham, progenitor of servants) operates for the master as a punitive reminder that the slave's identity is inextricably linked to his commodity status, regardless of intellectual or spiritual aspirations of the sort that originally distinguish Dave as a cultural leader.[14] But when Dave begins to identify too closely with the token of his degradation, becoming obsessed with hams to the point of madness, the master recognizes an impending threat to his pocketbook and has the shackles removed. Dave's liberation is a mixed blessing, however, for as Julius explains, "de ham had be'n on his neck so long dat Dave had sorter got use' ter it. He look des lack he'd los' sump'n fer a day er so atter de ham wuz tuk off, en didn' 'pear to know w'at ter do wid hisse'f" (131).

Unable to give up the symbol to which his identity has become firmly attached, Dave devises a pathetic substitute, tethering himself to a pine log when no one is looking in order to express what has become the inescapable sense of his reification. The tale concludes with a grisly pun, as Dave finally resorts to suicide in his search for a cure—in Julius's rendering, a "kyo"—for the psychological burden of enslavement. Julius comments that "Dave had kep' on gittin' wusser en wusser in his mine, 'tel he des got ter b'lievin' he wuz all done turnt ter a ham; en den he had gone en built a fier, en tied a rope roun' his neck, des lack de hams wuz tied, en had hung hisse'f up in de smoke-'ouse fer ter kyo" (134).

Robbed of his fledgling identity as a literate black man, coerced into identification with an inanimate object, then robbed again of the source of his reified slave identity, Dave is Chesnutt's most compelling example of a crippling postwar double bind, a case study of the enduring psychological effect of ethnic caricature upon its victims. The conjure element so common in Chesnutt's plantation tales has been replaced in "Dave's Neckliss" by a gruesome psychological realism, with the result that this account of human transformation lacks the "Oriental," fairy-tale quality of the stories collected in *The Conjure Woman*.[15] But the tale unfolds along a familiar boundary between the animate and inanimate worlds and registers symbolically not only the physical and intellectual degradation of human beings in bondage, but the power of ethnic misrepresentation as a disciplinary force that lives on long after emancipation in the minds of its subjects. As elsewhere in the dialect tales, the event of the slave's reification prepares the context for Chesnutt's more concentrated focus on the wrenching and only partly successful effort to shake off habits of mind formed under the duress of slavery: Tenie cannot rescue Sandy after his metamorphosis into a tree in "Po' Sandy"; Primus fails to regain human form in "The Conjurer's Re-

venge," remaining trapped in a suggestive dual existence, half man
and half mule; Dan in "The Gray Wolf's Ha'nt" is condemned to
live as a wolf after his failed restoration. Like Dave, each of these
characters suffers a two-fold human tragedy that subtly conflates the
twin indignities of chattelism and Jim Crow.

Yet to read "Dave's Neckliss" as an apology for the freedman's
intellectual shortcomings as a perpetual victim of slavery is to overlook Julius's investment in the story and its performance. As John
suggests in his opening comment, Julius's narrative habit of dwelling
on the antebellum past presents to the Northern couple "the curious
psychological spectacle" of an imagination enslaved long after the
physical shackles have been removed. John repeatedly draws this
conclusion about Julius's imaginative relation to the period "befo' de
wah," explaining in "Mars Jeems's Nightmare" that Julius "had been
unable to break off entirely the mental habits of a lifetime."[16] In "A
Victim of Heredity," John again rationalizes African-American behavior by asserting that several of his "dusky neighbors" "did not
shake off readily the habits formed under the old system."[17] According to John's view, Julius's commitment to the past, expressed in stories of plantation life, confirms his intellectual and imaginative limitation, leading John to doubt that Julius "even realized, except in a
vague, uncertain way, his own degradation" (125).

As a parable about the insufferable dilemma of a mind enslaved,
"Dave's Neckliss" would seem to offer symbolic confirmation for
John's beliefs, bearing out his view of Julius and other postwar
African Americans as the victims of persistent mental habits formed
under slavery. But of course in telling John exactly what John already
thinks he knows about his "dusky neighbors," Julius demonstrates
a level of self-consciousness that is inconsistent with John's theory
of mental habitude. In effect, the tale allegorizes Julius's own degradation as a legatee of the slave regime, fitting the ham-loving former slave neatly into a "coon" stereotype (Julius, like Dave, gazes
longingly at the ham on Annie's table in a suggestive act of identification); yet in apparently embracing John's condescending explanation for African-American shortcomings in the postwar era, Julius
assumes creative authority over Dave's and his own caricatured
image—the image of man as ham—revealing himself to be acutely
sensitive to the varieties of degradation suffered by blacks before and
after the war. As Sundquist cogently explains, "Dave's Neckliss" "rev-
els in the exploration of a culturally destructive image in order to appropriate its power in an act of figurative metamorphosis. Chesnutt's

fictive seizure of the image . . . is itself an act of cultural conjure that reclaims and transforms its significance."[18]

This "seizure" of the caricatured ethnic image is the decisive act of transformation in each of Chesnutt's tales of antebellum conjure and metamorphosis. Through his creative rendering of Dave's story, Uncle Julius inhabits John's demeaning image of the nostalgic former slave, mentally incapable of abandoning his former condition, even as he reveals the tragic attachment to stereotype as one aspect of his protagonist's degradation. The story's telling, in other words, both confirms and belies John's theory of the black "appurtenance," spelled out most thoroughly in "Mars Jeems's Nightmare," where John describes Julius's persistent habit of thinking of himself as an article belonging to the plantation.[19] Presumably like Dave, Julius simply cannot relinquish his former relation to white authority; yet his ability to narrate Dave's story—to allegorize self-consciously the tragic consequences of Dave's psychological enslavement—betrays Julius's highly cultivated performance of "coon" identity *as* a performance.

Chesnutt's finest dialect tales resemble "Dave's Neckliss" in their complex embrace of the reductive ethnic imagery he deplores, none more effectively than the minor masterpiece "A Victim of Heredity; or, Why the Darkey Loves Chicken."[20] The tale's overtly patronizing subtitle echoes such showstoppers as "Who Dat Say Chicken in Dis Crowd?," a popular "coon" song that plays on the standard representation of African Americans as irredeemable chicken thieves.[21] Julius narrates the story apparently in order to bear out his assertion that an appetite for chicken is "in the blood" of African Americans, who ought to be afforded "mo' lowance" for petty crimes committed out of hereditary compulsion (174). As in "Mars Jeems's Nightmare," where Julius cites "nachul bawn laz'ness" as the reason for his grandson's irresponsibility, here he welcomes the caricatured image of African Americans as naturally disposed to shiftless gluttony, arguing that "cullud folks is mo' fonder er chick'n 'n w'ite folks" because "dey can't he'p but be" (58, 174). Annie responds angrily to this demeaning account of African-American cultural difference, exclaiming "with some show of indignation" that Julius "ought to be ashamed to slander [his] race in that way" (174). Yet her indignation is characteristically overstated, for Annie fails to grasp Julius's probing critique of the "coon" symbolism his tale deploys for its own purposes.

Much like Chesnutt's better-known story "The Goophered Grapevine," this tale revolves around an acquisitive master's self-de-

feating effort to increase his wealth through the application of conjure to the plantation economy. Mars Donal' pays Aunt Peggy for a
goopher mixture that will control the appetite of his slaves so that he
can cut their rations without objection. He is so impressed with his
success, however, that he applies a catastrophic second dose, reducing his slaves to invalids. As a convalescent measure, Aunt Peggy rec-
ommends a steady diet of chicken, which Mars Donal' provides
at ruinous expense to himself. Peggy finally concocts an antidote
that will restore the appetite of his slaves, but not before Mars
Donal' has squandered his wealth. Moreover, she explains that the
goopher was applied so carelessly that "its got in dey blood . . .
[s]o I 'spec's you'll hatter gib yo' niggers chick'n at leas' oncet a week
ez long ez dey libs, ef you wanter git de wuk out'n 'em dat you
oughter" (181). Julius concludes by theorizing that "dey wuz so many
niggers on ole Mars Donal's plantation . . . en dey got scattered
roun' so befo' de wah en sence, dat dey ain' ha'dly no cullu'd folks in
No'f Ca'lina but w'at's got some er de blood er dem goophered niggers in dey vames. En so eber sence den, all de niggers in No'f
Ca'lina has ter hab chick'n at leas' oncet er week fer ter keep dey
healt' en strenk. En dat's w'y cullu'd folks laks chick'n mo' d'n w'ite
folks" (181).

Rather than argue for the innate equality of the races by rooting
out an offensive cultural fiction, Julius demands that the "coon"
image, so prominently featured in song and illustration throughout
the late nineteenth century, is indelibly scripted "in the blood."
Annie initially objects to the degrading logic of this plea for leniency,
much as she upbraids Julius for his apparent self-deprecation in
"The Conjurer's Revenge." But Annie's egalitarian instincts are misguided here, in the same way that Amiri Baraka is at least half wrong
when he identifies Chesnutt with a slave mentality that seeks "to lose
itself" completely in "the culture of the ex-master," for Julius insists
on the "influence of heredity" as a way of appropriating a racist fiction and making it his own.[22] Tangling accommodationist and subversive gestures with every word he speaks, Julius manages to gratify
John's worst assumptions about African-American inferiority by arguing that blacks are naturally compelled to steal chicken, while at
the same time maintaining that this "natural" disposition is entirely
traceable to environmental conditions linked to slavery and postwar
racism. Although Aunt Peggy's goopher is forever dispersed in the
blood of former slaves, leaving them uniquely susceptible to criminal
temptation, Mars Donal' is the one responsible for putting it there.

Thus despite the story's offensively reductive account of African-American racial traits inherited from the era "befo' de wah," heredity and environment are finally made to seem like interchangeable and indistinguishable terms. The stereotype may be "in the blood," according to Julius's parable, but only in the sense that black blood is part of a larger cultural fiction constructed by whites to serve the continuing project of oppression.

Although for many readers, including myself, Chesnutt's art achieves its greatest effect in such muted forms of protest and creative appropriation, he was understandably troubled by his own role in perpetuating the conventions of "coon" comedy. Indeed, although the dialect stories consistently reveal the "intensely human inner life of slavery," as John puts it in "Dave's Neckliss," they begin and end with an assertion of stark intellectual inequality. Moreover, rather than disrupt the linguistic hierarchy in which Julius's narratives occupy a subordinate place, Chesnutt's dialect tales typically end by reaffirming John's authority over the plantation and its inhabitants. If the former slave's manipulation of ethnic clichés represents a form of resistance, it is one John has no trouble ignoring, and Chesnutt himself seems resigned to admit that such resistance does little or nothing to bridge the gap between John's and Julius's mutually exclusive social worlds.

Chesnutt understood from the outset that stories about "Why the Darkey Loves Chicken," however ingeniously subversive they might be, did not serve the "high, holy purpose" of his writing career, which was—as he explained to himself in an 1880 journal entry—"to accustom the public mind to the idea" of "the negro's . . . social recognition and equality."[23] Determined to write a more socially progressive form of fiction, he announced his decision in 1889 to abandon "the old Negro who serves as mouthpiece . . . as well as much of the dialect."[24] He would later return to Uncle Julius and the plantation formula at the urging of his editor at Houghton Mifflin, Walter Hines Page, but throughout most of the 1890s—a decade that saw the rise of the "coon show" and an explosion of interest in ethnic humor throughout popular culture—Chesnutt bucked the trend. "Groveland," a fictional version of the mixed-race, middle-class, urban world to which Chesnutt himself belonged, became the site of his most ambitious efforts to tease out the intricacies of life along the color line, where Chesnutt believed the "future American type" was in the process of emerging. "Darky" humor of the sort he understood all too well no longer contributed directly to the design of Chesnutt's fictional world, and yet the logic of ethnic caricature—even in its formal absence—continued to inform his literary imagination in decisive ways.

In certain respects, the distance that separates John's plantation in "Patesville," North Carolina, from the midwestern city of Groveland cannot be measured in miles, for these fictional settings and the characters who inhabit them are worlds apart. Indeed, although Uncle Julius's imagination can be characterized by its absorption in past relations, which "clung to his mind, like barnacles to the submerged portion of a ship," the central character in "The Wife of His Youth" (1898), one of Chesnutt's most intriguing color-line stories, has effectively banished all traces of his Southern past from consciousness.[25] As a leading member of Groveland's exclusive mixed-race society of "Blue Veins," Mr. Ryder shares the group's idealized conception of whiteness and, although not a founding member himself, emerges as the society's principal custodian of "standards" based entirely on skin color (3). His "genius for social leadership" facilitates the massive repression of all that the group "collectively disclaimed," namely blackness and the legacy of African-American slavery (3). Ryder's pursuit of a racial fantasy, expressed in his admiration for Tennyson's "A Dream of Fair Women," promises to culminate with his marriage to Mrs. Dixon, a woman who is "whiter than he and better educated" (5). Their union, he reasons, will further guarantee his eventual "absorption by the white race," a process he defends with an ironic allusion to the Great Emancipator: " 'With malice towards none, with charity for all,' we must do the best we can for ourselves and those who are to follow us. Self-preservation is the first law of nature" (7).

Before he can realize his dream, however, Ryder is faced with a moral and psychological dilemma when the long-forgotten wife of his youth arrives at his doorstep in search of her husband, whom she describes as "a merlatter man by de name er Sam Taylor" (11). Immediately recognizing her as the woman he married down South, prior to his personal transformation, Ryder marvels that this "bit of the old plantation" appears to have been "summoned up from the past by the wave of a magician's wand," but it would be more accurate to say that Liza Jane has been summoned by the wave of a caricaturist's pen (10). Her ethnicity is deeply inscribed in the "hundred wrinkles" that "crossed and re-crossed" her dark face, in the "ancient" costume she wears, and in the tufts of "short gray wool" that protrude from her faded bonnet (10). With "kindly patronage" that barely conceals his disgust, Ryder invites the woman to sit down and tell her story, which is delivered in a tortured dialect and serves to emphasize the impression he has already formed, namely that "she was very black" (10–11).

As Werner Sollers has explained, Liza Jane is not a character but an essence, a racial principle signifying "the world of *descent*" for a culture that denies its authority over social life.[26] Indeed, her withered black form is constructed out of the same visual clichés that constituted black identity on the "coon show" stage, and in important respects Chesnutt's story derives its narrative impulse from the logic of "coon" comedy: after a misguided attempt to conceal his race origin, Ryder is reminded of who he *really* is and must remain, for a "coon" can never become anything but a "coon." Liza Jane's cartoon image, as Sollers points out, closely resembles that of Gitl, the Jewish wife in Abraham Cahan's *Yekl: A Tale of the New York Ghetto*, who presents a similarly "grotesque" reminder of the protagonist's ethnic origin when she arrives at Ellis Island: "She was naturally dark of complexion, and the nine or ten days spent at sea had covered her face with a deep bronze, which combined with her prominent cheek bones, inky little eyes, and, above all, the smooth black wig, to lend her resemblance to a squaw."[27]

To the male protagonists of "Yekl" and "The Wife of His Youth," the caricatured ethnic image symbolizes the inassimilable strangeness of ethnic origin, and yet for both Cahan and Chesnutt this return of the culturally repressed signals the beginning, rather than the end, of meaningful cultural synthesis. If "coon" songs of the period ritually enacted the spectacle of failed assimilation, affirming that figures marked by ethnicity remain irreparably alien, Cahan and Chesnutt deploy the same leaden symbolism to explore the pathologies that drive their protagonists toward extremes of denial and self-loathing. For both writers, the inevitable process of cultural blending—or "amalgamation," to use Chesnutt's preferred term—begins with a charged confrontation between old and new structures of identity, which stand out in high relief only until more fundamental continuities, rooted in shared human nature, become apparent. In fact, although Cahan's Yiddish "squaw" may stand for everything foreign to Yekl's American experience, her racially marked eyes, cheeks, skin, and hair already embody a complex blending of ethnic cues (is she of Native-American, Hebrew, or perhaps Asian origin?), to the point that her caricatured image operates for Yekl as a symbol race itself, rather than of any one race in particular. His rejection of her is a rejection of ethnicity, much as Ryder's Tennysonian "Dream of Fair Women" imagines his "absorption by the white race" as a cleansing process, one ultimately consistent with the fantasy of "Anglo-Saxon" racial integrity.

Of course, Chesnutt considered this fantasy a major obstacle to the natural "formation of a uniform type out of our present racial elements," and Ryder has the good fortune to awaken from his delusion in time to act accordingly. At a lavish dinner party, intended to celebrate his proposal to Mrs. Dixon, he presents his dilemma as a hypothetical question to his fellow Blue Veins, dropping into a "soft dialect, which came readily to his lips," to deliver Liza Jane's tale (20). As if collectively awakened from their pursuit of a false ideal, the dinner guests react with a "responsive thrill" to Ryder's narration, unanimously joining Mrs. Dixon in affirming the husband's responsibility to his past (20). Having evidently reached the same decision himself, Ryder happily accepts the group's verdict and acknowledges Liza Jane as the wife of his youth.

The significance of this decision is worth pausing over, for in important respects it is no decision at all. The story breaks off immediately after Ryder's seemingly momentous embrace of the past, and yet Chesnutt leaves it unclear whether Ryder's acknowledgement of Liza Jane implies a renewal of their antebellum marriage vows, or simply an enlargement of his moral vision. Because, as a slave, Liza Jane was not eligible to enter into a binding civil contract, their marriage bears no legal force at the moment of his dramatic revelation, and indeed Ryder is careful to introduce her not as "my wife" (which, in a legal sense, she is not), but as "the wife of my youth" (24). His parsing of words might actually be understood as a way of claiming a measure of independence from responsibilities that attach to his former identity, rather than to himself. My point is not to suggest that Ryder's climactic gesture is insincere, but that Chesnutt achieves an almost Howellsian level of ambivalence in having it both ways: Ryder breaks the spell of race consciousness in himself and others by acknowledging the claim of racial essence upon his sense of identity; or, to put the paradox more plainly, Ryder's acknowledgement of an ethnic origin is at once limiting and liberating, in that it frees him to marry Mrs. Dixon for the right reasons and, in doing so, promises to bring about the racial "amalgamation" that Chesnutt saw as necessary and desirable. I have been arguing throughout these pages that ethnic caricature supplied the late nineteenth century's most effective vocabulary for articulating the paradoxical view that identity originates simultaneously in a universal source of human "character"—Howells's term for the shared psychic or spiritual material that underlies individuality—*and* in race-specific tendencies that differentiate the various ethnic "types." Chesnutt's personal investment in issues of racial justice makes him appear exceptional among such contemporaries as Howells, Twain, James, and Wharton, and yet he employed ethnic caricature to express the same fundamental ambivalence. Liza Jane's explicitly racialized image, with its trappings of "coon" convention, allows Ryder to claim an ethnic origin while being released from the stigma it imposes.

This reading of Ryder's decision suggests a useful parallel with "Dave's Neckliss," where the plot dilemma arises not from a lack, but from a crippling excess, of cultural memory. Whereas Dave—through Julius's highly motivated narration—presents the degraded "spectacle of a mind enslaved," Ryder exemplifies a different kind of degradation (for Chesnutt, one no less profound), which occurs when identity becomes perfectly detached from cultural sources and communal relations. As a character who has so successfully negotiated the transition to a new identity that he does not at first even recognize the token of his Southern past, Ryder might be understood as Dave's psychological antithesis. Unflattering as the comparison must seem to Liza Jane, she performs exactly the same function as the ham in "Dave's Neckliss," offering through her caricatured image a symbolic point of reference for the protagonist's developing postwar identity. Dave is destroyed by his perfect identification with the symbol of his reification under slavery, whereas Ryder is threatened by his perfect detachment from a former identity, that of Liza Jane's antebellum husband. Chesnutt implies through Dave's suicide and Ryder's ambivalent choice that a viable conception of identity must be tied to the ethnic past and unencumbered by it at the same time. Julius strikes such a precarious balance when he performs stories about chicken thieves, mules, and "mulattos," stories in which ethnic caricature serves to dramatize the simultaneous recovery of, and release from, a reified conception of racial essence. Ryder may have little in common with Julius as a performer, but his delivery of Liza Jane's narrative achieves the same precarious balance.

As I hope I have successfully demonstrated already, the double movement that allows Chesnutt to have his ethnic cake and eat it, too, is a Howellsian gesture *par excellence*. In fact, it is the defining

gesture of American realism in the domain of ethnic characterization. Reviewing Chesnutt's stories for the *Atlantic Monthly* in 1900,
Howells claimed to have discovered a kindred spirit, and he eagerly
acknowledged the younger writer's membership in "the good school,
the only school, all aberrations from nature being so much truancy
and anarchy."[28] Howells admired Chesnutt's "passionless handling"
of a subject "tense with potential tragedy," noting that the narrative
voice of the color line stories remains at once detached and yet intri-
cately engaged with its subject (52). For Howells, such "artistic reti-
cence" betrayed the hand of a true realist, a writer capable of show-
ing, as Howells elsewhere explains, that "human nature is the same
in all environments," regardless of the "masks and disguises that
novel conditions have put upon it" (53).[29]

    Such a ringing endorsement should cause no surprise, for in im-
portant respects Chesnutt's social vision coincided exactly with the
democratic impulse of Howellsian realism. Chesnutt's faith in "the
essential unity of the human race," as both an anthropological fact
and a future social condition, explicitly echoed Howells's belief in
"the equality of things and the unity of men," a principle that constituted, for Howells, "the solidarity of all the arts, and the universality
of fiction."[30] Howells insisted that Chesnutt's characters compel interest not because of their ethnicity, but because of their humanity,
which invites the discerning reader to discover "himself, his motives,
principles, passions, reflected in people of a wholly different tradition and physiognomy." Such moments of transgressive identification produce, in Howells's understanding of literature, "the chief delight that an author can give the reader."[31]

    Howells may have recognized in Chesnutt's stories an expression
of his own fraternal vision of mankind, but he did not share Chesnutt's conclusion that amalgamation is the inevitable tendency of a
heterogeneous society. Although fiction may open channels of imaginative sympathy between the "types" of mankind, Howells was reluctant to abandon ethnic typology altogether, either in his own
fiction—as we have seen—or in that of the "ethnic writers" he problematically championed as a critic. His enthusiasm for Dunbar's poetry
is a case in point. In a famous essay, Howells praised Dunbar's poems
as "evidence of the essential unity of the human race, which does not
think or feel black in one and white in another, but humanly in all."[32]
Yet this inclusive gesture is immediately followed by the observation
that "there is a precious difference of temperament between the races
which it would be a great pity ever to lose" (280). Moreover, according

to Howells, this essential race-quality "is best preserved and most charmingly suggested by Mr. Dunbar in those pieces of his where he studies the moods and traits of his race in its own accent of our English" (280). Race is a fiction, the essay declares, and yet to abandon the defining force of ethnic stigmas, especially those that treat "the negro's limitations" with sympathy and humor, would be a "great pity" (280). For the "ethnic writers" whose careers Howells brokered from the "Editor's Study" at *Harper's*—including Chesnutt, Dunbar, Cahan, and Boyesen—membership in "the good school" required mastery of this circular maneuver, in which ethnicity is understood to be perfectly irrelevant and all-important at the same time.

In praising Chesnutt's stories of the color line, Howells issued a similarly double-edged prescription for "ethnic writing" in the realist vein. Chesnutt's mixed-race characters exemplify the realist credo that "human nature is the same in all environments," for they invite the reader's identification at the level of shared human experience, where ethnicity reveals itself as a mere disguise. But this disguise is curiously decisive in Chesnutt's rendering of mixed-race identity, according to Howells, who goes on to observe that "it *is* their negro blood that excludes them," and that binds them "in that sad solidarity from which there is no hope of entrance into polite white society" (54, emphasis added). Like Dunbar's dialect poems, Chesnutt's stories uncover the fiction of race only to confirm that race remains the defining feature of the social world about which he writes. In touching these two discordant notes at once, Chesnutt's finest work achieves, in Howells's view, a "curious realism," which might in fact be understood as nothing more curious than American realism from an "ethnic" point of view. The color line stories allow readers of all races and cultures to enter imaginatively into "those regions where the paler shades dwell," and yet such transgressive identification only confirms for Howells that Chesnutt's "middle world" lies "wholly outside our own," and that his characters dwell there "as hopelessly, with relation to ourselves, as the blackest negro" (54).

Howells has been criticized for offering praise on such terms, but he saw clearly what representational game Chesnutt was playing, and the subtly constraining logic of his review only reproduced Chesnutt's own ambivalence in the act of praising it. Chesnutt expressed nothing but gratitude for Howells's influential remarks, and yet the essentialist underpinning of the review must have persuaded him—if he needed persuading—that this was a game the "ethnic writer" could not win. Indeed, from the moment he determined to abandon black dialect as a literary device, Chesnutt understood that "realism" of the sort promoted by men such as Howells and Richard Watson Gilder of *Century* was incompatible with his vision of social reality.[33] Throughout most of his short and spectacular career, however, Chesnutt excelled at "playing the races," which is to say that he marshaled the resources of ethnic caricature in the service of literary realism. The particular quality of his ambivalence about the role of ethnicity in the larger structure of identity may have been unique among major writers of the period, but like Howells, Twain, James, and Wharton, Chesnutt discovered a form for the expression of his ambivalence in the distorted features of the exaggerated ethnic image.

NOTES

INTRODUCTION

1. There exists a voluminous critical literature on the demeaning representation of black subjects in American art, literature, and music. Some of the most useful sources for this study include: Joseph Boskin, *Sambo: The Rise and Demise of an American Jester* (New York: Oxford University Press, 1986); George M. Fredrickson, *The Black Image in the White Mind: The Debate on Afro-American Character and Destiny, 1817–1914* (Middletown, Conn.: Wesleyan University Press, 1971); Jean Fagan Yellin, *The Intricate Knot: Black Figures in American Literature, 1776–1863* (New York: New York University Press, 1972); Sterling A. Brown, *The Negro in American Fiction* (1937; reprint, New York: Atheneum, 1969); Seymour L. Gross and John Edward Hardy, eds., *Images of the Negro in American Literature* (Chicago: University of Chicago Press, 1966); and Jan Nederveen Pieterse, *White on Black: Images of Africa and Blacks in Western Popular Culture* (New Haven, Conn.: Yale University Press, 1992).

2. Quoted in Albert Boime, *The Art of Exclusion: Representing Blacks in the Nineteenth Century* (Washington, D.C.: Smithsonian Institution Press, 1990), 36.

3. Ibid., 102.

4. Ibid., 5.

5. Alice Walker, "Introduction" to *Ethnic Notions: Black Images in the White Mind: An Exhibition of Afro-American Stereotype and Caricature from the Collection of Janette Faulkner* (Berkeley, Calif.: Berkeley Art Center Association, 1982), 11.

6. Quoted in Karen Adams, "Black Images in Nineteenth-Century American Painting and Literature: An Iconological Study of Mount,

Melville, Homer, and Mark Twain" (Ph.D. diss., Emory University, 1978), 48.

7. William Dean Howells, *Selected Literary Criticism, Volume 2: 1886–1897,* ed. Donald Pizer et al. (Bloomington: Indiana University Press, 1993), 353.

8. Kenneth W. Warren, *Black and White Strangers: Race and American Literary Realism* (Chicago: University of Chicago Press, 1993), 52.

9. Alain Locke, "American Literary Tradition and the Negro," in *The Critical Temper of Alain Locke: A Selection of His Essays on Art and Culture,* ed. Jeffrey C. Stewart (New York: Garland Publishing, 1983), 438.

10. Alain Locke, "The Saving Grace of Realism," in *The Critical Temper of Alain Locke,* 222.

11. Erich Auerbach, *Mimesis: The Representation of Reality in Western Literature,* trans. Willard R. Trask (Princeton, N.J.: Princeton University Press, 1953), 552.

12. Thomas Sergeant Perry, "William Dean Howells," *Century* 23 (March 1882): 683–84.

13. See J. Stanley Lemons, "Black Stereotypes as Reflected in Popular Culture, 1880–1920," *American Quarterly* 29 (Spring 1977): 102–16.

14. Boime, *The Act of Exclusion,* 98–99.

15. Quoted in Boime, *The Act of Exclusion,* 99.

16. Quoted in Adams, "Black Images in Nineteenth-Century American Painting and Literature," 135.

17. Ibid.

18. Henry Fielding, "Author's Preface" to *Joseph Andrews* (1742; rpt. Middletown, Conn.: Wesleyan University Press, 1967), xxxix.

19. Hogarth's didactic engraving from 1743, exhibiting "a farther Explanation of the Difference Betwixt Character and Caricatura," is reproduced in William Feaver's *Masters of Caricature* (New York: Alfred E. Knopf, 1981), 15.

20. Howells, *Selected Literary Criticism,* vol. 2, 303.

21. Ibid., 353.

22. Mark Twain, *Adventures of Huckleberry Finn* (1885; reprint, Berkeley: University of California Press, 1985), 269. It seems noteworthy in this context to point out that Twain actually gives Huck's interior voice a speaking part within the text, further emphasizing the reality and independence of the private self.

23. Quoted in Beverly R. David, "Visions of the South: Joel Chandler Harris and His Illustrators," *American Literary Realism* (Summer 1976): 198.

24. Quoted in Ernst Gombrich, *Caricature* (Middlesex, UK: King, Penguin, 1940), 14.

25. Gombrich and Ernst Kris, "The Principle of Caricature," *British Journal of Medical Psychology* 18 (1938): 322.

26. Robert de la Sizeranne, "What Is Caricature?" *Littel's Living Age* 221 (April 1899): 86.

27. Ibid., 8.

28. Quoted in Miles Orvell, *The Real Thing: Imitation and Authenticity in American Culture, 1880–1940* (Chapel Hill: University of North Carolina Press, 1989), 38.

29. Twain's fascination with communication technology is an important theme in all of the major biographies, including Albert Bigelow Paine's *Mark Twain: A Biography,* 4 vols. (New York: Harper & Brothers, 1912), Justin Kaplan's *Mr. Clemens and Mark Twain* (New York: Simon & Schuster, 1966), and Andrew Hoffman's *Inventing Mark Twain: The Life of Samuel Langhorne Clemens* (New York: William Morrow, 1997). Of particular interest in this connection is also Alan Gribben's essay, "Mark Twain, Phrenology, and the 'Temperaments': A Study of Pseudoscientific Influence," *American Quarterly* 24 (March 1972): 45–68.

30. Among other examples, one thinks immediately of the duke in *Adventures of Huckleberry Finn,* who takes "at turn at mesmerism and phrenology when there's a chance" (*Huckleberry Finn,* 162).

31. For discussions of the relationship between caricature and academic physiognomy, see Edward Lucie-Smith, *The Art of Caricature* (Ithaca, N.Y.: Cornell University Press, 1981), Thomas Wright, *A History of Caricature and Grotesque in Literature and Art* (1865; reprint, New York: Frederick Ungar, 1968), and Feaver, *Masters of Caricature.*

32. Ernest Hogan, "The Phrenologist Coon," Department of Special Collections, Knight Library, University of Oregon.

33. *Scribner's Monthly* became *Century Illustrated Monthly* when Richard Watson Gilder took over the magazine's editorship in 1881. *Scribner's Magazine* began publishing in 1887. Some of the illustrated weeklies that emerged after 1850 included *Gleason's Pictorial Drawing-Room Companion,* the *Illustrated American News, Frank Leslie's Illustrated Paper,* the *New York Illustrated News,* and *Harper's Weekly.* For a thorough history of early magazine publishing, see Frank Luther Mott, *A History of American Magazines, Vol. 1: 1741–1850* (New York: Appleton, 1930).

34. William Dean Howells, *A Hazard of New Fortunes* (1890; reprint, New York: Oxford University Press, 1990), 7.

35. Henry James, *Picture and Text* (New York: Harper & Brothers, 1903) 1. Clara Marburg Kirk contends that Howells's decision to leave the *Atlantic* was based in part on its refusal to "follow the trend toward the illustrated magazine." *W. D. Howells in His Time* (New Brunswick, N.J.: Rutgers University Press, 1965), 65. For an excellent discussion of Howells's and James's attitudes toward illustration, see also Teona Tone Gneiting, "Picture and Text: A Theory of Illustrated Fiction in

the Nineteenth Century" (Ph.D. diss., University of California, Los Angeles, 1977).

36. For a contemporary account of these developments, see Algeron Tassin, *The Magazine in America* (New York: Dodd, Mead, 1916), especially chapters 13–14.

37. Richard Ohmann, *Selling Culture: Magazines, Markets, and Class at the Turn of the Century* (London: Verso, 1996), 25.

38. Quoted in Tassin, *The Magazine in America*, 353.

39. It is perhaps surprising that *Munsey's, Cosmopolitan,* and *McClure's* featured significantly fewer graphic caricatures, including crude ethnic images, than their more up-scale counterparts. Although humorous ethnic misrepresentations carried broad appeal with the mass-audience these newer magazines helped to create, the relatively high cost of employing original artists may have given the older periodicals an advantage in this emerging form of low-brow humor.

40. Frank Luther Mott, *A History of American Magazines, vol. 4: 1885–1905* (Cambridge, Mass.: Harvard University Press, 1957), 559.

41. Arthur Penn, "The Growth of Caricature," *The Critic* 2 (December 1882): 49–50; John Addington Symonds, "Caricature, the Fantastic, the Grotesque," *Littell's Living Age* 177 (April–June 1888): 344–49; J. A. Mitchell, "Contemporary American Caricature," *Scribner's* 6 (July–December 1889): 728–45; Joseph B. Bishop, "Early Political Caricature in America," *Century* 44 (1891): 219–31; Harold Payne, "Our Caricaturists and Cartoonists," *Munsey's Magazine* 10 (February 1894): 538–50; Henry McBride, "Technical Tendencies of Caricature," *Quarterly Illustrator* 4 (May 1995); "Moral Reflections on Burlesque Art," *Quarterly Illustrator* 5 (July 1895); and Robert de la Sizeranne, "What Is Caricature?," *Littell's Living Age* 221 (April 1899): 1–11, 86–98.

42. Henry James, "Daumier, Caricaturist," *Century* 39 (September 1890): 402–13.

43. Newell's images of comical African Americans also appeared in *Century,* in one case as a graphic companion to Paul Laurence Dunbar's dialect poem, "A Coquette Conquered," *Century* 52 (July 1896): 479.

44. Henry McBride, "Technical Tendencies of Caricature," *Quarterly Illustrator* 4 (May 1995): np.

45. Ohmann, *Selling Culture*, 7.

46. Quoted in Tassin, *The Magazine in America*, 342.

47. Quoted in Christopher Wilson, "The Rhetoric of Consumption: Mass-Market Magazines and the Demise of the Gentle Reader, 1880–1920," in *The Culture of Consumption: Critical Essays in American History, 1880–1980,* eds. Richard Wightman Fox and T. J. Jackson Lears (New York: Pantheon, 1983), 49.

48. Quoted in Theodore Peterson, *Magazines in the Twentieth Century* (Urbana: University of Illinois Press, 1964), 15.

49. Wilson, "The Rhetoric of Consumption," 49.

50. Howells, *Selected Literary Criticism,* vol. 2, 353.

51. Howells, *Editor's Study,* ed. James W. Simpson (Troy, N.Y.: Whitson, 1983), 169.

52. Howells, *Selected Literary Criticism,* vol. 2, 300.

53. Ibid., 321.

54. Amy Kaplan, *The Social Construction of American Realism* (Chicago: University of Chicago Press, 1988), especially chapter two on "The Mass-mediated Realism of William Dean Howells," 15–43.

55. Roswell Smith, letter to Howells, March 17, 1885, reprinted in *The Rise of Silas Lapham,* ed. Don L. Cook (1885; reprint, New York: W. W. Norton, 1982), 377.

56. L. Perry Curtis, Jr., describes the long tradition of British caricatures of the Irish in *Apes and Angels: The Irishman in Victorian Caricature* (Washington, D.C.: Smithsonian Institution Press, 1971). The extension of this tradition in American magazines and weekly papers is examined by John J. Appel in "From Shanties to Lace Curtains: The Irish Image in *Puck,* 1876–1910," *Comparative Studies in Society and History* 13 (October 1971).

57. For concise histories of these magazines and their numerous contemporaries, see David E. E. Sloane, *American Humor Magazines and Comic Periodicals* (New York: Garland Publishing, 1987).

58. Roger A. Fischer discusses the political sympathies of the major comic periodicals in *Them Damn Pictures: Explorations in American Political Cartoon Art* (North Haven, Conn.: Archon Books, 1996).

59. Fischer explains that Nast's representation of the Tweed gang as a violent ring of "Neanderthal Irish hooligans" was itself a gross distortion, "because the Irish were still only junior partners in the organization, and ['Slippery Dick'] Connolly and ['Brains'] Sweeney were the only Hibernians among the notables," *Them Damned Pictures,* 10.

60. T. Jackson Lears, *No Place of Grace: Antimodernism and the Transformation of American Culture, 1880–1929* (New York: Pantheon, 1981), and Tom Lutz, *American Nervousness, 1903: An Anecdotal History* (Ithaca, N.Y.: Cornell University Press, 1991).

61. In addition to the more general sources listed in note 1, the following titles provide useful information on "coon" representation in American popular culture: Lemons, "Black Stereotypes as Reflected in Popular Culture, 1880–1920"; James Dornan, "Shaping the Popular Image of Post Reconstruction American Blacks: The 'Coon Song' Phenomenon of the Gilded Age," *American Quarterly* 40 (December 1988): 450–71; Sam Dennison, *Scandalize My Name: Black American Imagery in*

American Popular Music (New York: Garland Publishing, 1982); Donald Bogle, *Toms, Coons, Mulattoes, and Bucks: An Interpretive History of Blacks in American Films* (New York: Viking, 1973); and Kathleen Leah Cothern, "The Coon Song: A Study of American Music, Entertainment, and Racism," (masters thesis, University of Oregon, 1990).

62. Patterns of anti-Semitic caricature in America are the subject of numerous books and articles, the most important of which for this study include Harley Erdman, *Staging the Jew: The Performance of an American Ethnic Identity, 1860–1920* (New Brunswick, N.J.: Rutgers University Press, 1997); John J. Appel, "Jews in American Caricature, 1820–1914," *American Jewish History* 71 (September 1981): 103–33; Rudolph Glanz, *The Jew in Early American Wit and Graphic Humor* (New York: KTAV Publishing, 1973); Oscar Handlin, "American Views of the Jew at the Opening of the Twentieth Century," *Publications of the American Jewish Historical Society* 40 (June 1951): 324–45; John Higham, *Strangers in the Land: Patterns of American Nativism, 1860–1925* (New Brunswick, N.J.: Rutgers University Press, 1955); and Michael N. Dobkowski, *The Tarnished Dream: The Basis of American Anti-Semitism* (Westport, Conn.: Greenwood Press, 1979). Equally helpful, though more general in focus, are Walter Benn Michaels, *Our America: Nativism, Modernism, Pluralism* (Durham, N.C.: Duke University Press, 1995); Sander Gillman, *The Jew's Body* (New York: Routledge, 1991) and *Difference and Pathology* (Ithaca, N.Y.: Cornell University Press, 1985); Michael Rogin, "Blackface, White Noise: The Jewish Jazz Singer Finds His Voice," *Critical Inquiry* 18 (1992): 125–34, and "Making America Home: Racial Masquerade and Ethnic Assimilation in the Transition to Talking Pictures," *Journal of American History* 79 (1992): 1050–77.

63. Robert B. Fletcher, "Visual Thinking and the Picture Story in *The History of Henry Esmond*," *Publication of the Modern Language Association* (*PMLA*) 113 (May 1998): 381.

64. Gombrich and Kris, "The Principle of Caricature," 324.

65. Anna Julia Cooper challenged Howells's use of African-American stereotypes in *An Imperative Duty* by exclaiming, "Mr. Howells does not know what he is talking about" (*A Voice from the South* [1892; reprint, New York: Oxford University Press, 1988], 201). More recent critics have often repeated this general explanation for the annoying presence of caricature and racial stereotype in realist fiction. See, for example, Warner Berthoff, *The Ferment of Realism: American Literature, 1884–1919* (New York: Macmillan, 1965); Jay Martin, *Harvests of Change: American Literature, 1865–1914* (Englewood Cliffs, N.J.: Prentice-Hall, 1967); and Larzer Ziff, *The American 1890s: Life and Times of a Lost Generation* (Lincoln: University of Nebraska Press, 1966).

66. June Howard, *Form and History in American Literary Naturalism* (Chapel Hill: University of North Carolina Press, 1985), especially chapter 3, "Casting Out the Outcast: Naturalism and the Brute," 70–103.

67. Kaplan, *The Social Construction of American Realism*, 9–10.

68. William Dean Howells, *An Imperative Duty*, ed. David J. Nordloh, et al. (1891; reprint, Bloomington: Indiana University Press, 1970), 6–7.

69. Werner Sollors, *Beyond Ethnicity: Consent and Descent in American Culture* (New York: Oxford University Press, 1986), hereafter cited within the text.

70. In fact, Sollors reproduces a telling image from *Puck* ("The Mortar of Assimilation," June 26, 1889) to illustrate his argument.

71. Michael North, *The Dialect of Modernism: Race, Language, and Twentieth-Century Literature* (New York: Oxford University Press, 1994).

72. Ernest Hemingway, *The Sun Also Rises* (1926; rpt. New York: Simon & Schuster, 1987), 69; Willa Cather, *My Antonia* (1918; reprint, New York: Penguin, 1994), 144; William Faulkner, *The Sound and the Fury* (1929; reprint, New York: Norton, 1994), 55.

CHAPTER I

1. William Dean Howells, "Criticism and Fiction," in *Selected Literary Criticism, vol. 2: 1886–1897*, ed. David J. Nordloh et al. (Bloomington: Indiana University Press, 1993), 301. Parenthetical references in this and the following paragraph are to this edition of "Criticism and Fiction."

2. Howells, "My Literary Passions," in *Selected Literary Criticism, vol. 2: 1886–1897*, ed. David J. Nordloh et al. (Bloomington: Indiana University Press, 1993), 261–62.

3. Ibid., 163.

4. Howells, "My Favorite Novelist and His Best Book," in *Selected Literary Criticism, vol. 2: 1886–1897*, 283.

5. Howells, "Henry James, Jr.," in *W. D. Howells as Critic*, ed. Edwin H. Cady (Boston: Routledge & Kegan Paul, 1973), 71.

6. Howells, "My Favorite Novelist and His Best Book," 283.

7. Howells, "Concerning a Council of Imperfection," *Literature* 1 (April 7, 1899), 290.

8. Howells, *The Editor's Study*, ed. James W. Simpson (Troy, N.Y.: Whitson, 1983), 22.

9. Howells, "Criticism and Fiction," 353–54.

10. Ibid., 353.

11. "Editor's Drawer," *Harper's Monthly* 77 (November 1888), 970.

12. Howells, "My Literary Passions," 263.

13. Howells, "Criticism and Fiction," 330. Parenthetical references in this and the following paragraph are to the Indiana University Press edition of "Criticism and Fiction."

14. Howells, *A Hazard of New Fortunes,* ed. David J. Nordloh, et al. (Bloomington: Indiana University Press, 1970), 183. Subsequent references to this edition appear within the text. Elsa Nettles discusses this paradox as a common feature of realist experiments with ethnic dialect in *Language, Race, and Social Class in Howells's America* (Lexington: University of Kentucky Press, 1988). See especially her excellent chapters 4–6 on "Realism and Dialect," "The Problem of 'Negro Dialect' in Literature," and "Language, Race, and Nationality in Howells's Fiction."

15. Holger Kersten explores the conventions of ethnic caricature as they apply to the representation of German immigrants in a fine essay, "Using the Immigrant's Voice: Humor and Pathos in Nineteenth Century 'Dutch' Dialect Texts," *MELUS* 21 (Winter 1996): 3–17.

16. Nettles, *Language, Race, and Social Class in Howells's America,* 95.

17. Henry James, *The Portrait of a Lady* (1908; reprint, London: Penguin, 1986), 110.

18. Ibid., 114.

19. Ibid., 116.

20. Howells, *The Rise of Silas Lapham* in *Novels 1875–1886* (New York: Library of America, 1982), 867. Subsequent references to this edition are provided in the text.

21. Phillip Barrish, *American Literary Realism, Critical Theory, and Intellectual Prestige, 1880–1995* (Cambridge: Cambridge University Press, 2001), 25.

22. Ibid..

23. Ibid., 29.

24. Howells, *The World of Chance: A Novel* (New York: Harper, 1893), 129. Quoted in Barrish, 34.

25. Howells, "A Pedestrian Tour," in *Suburban Sketches* (1871; reprint, Boston: James R. Osgood, 1872), 71, 68. Subsequent references to this edition are provided in the text. Walter Benn Michaels discusses the radical nativist thinking of Grant's *The Passing of the Great Race* and Stoddard's *Re-Forging America* in *Our America: Nativism, Modernism, and Pluralism* (Durham, N.C.: Duke University Press, 1995).

26. Howells's contemporary, Anna Julia Cooper, objected to his representation of African Americans as simple-minded, dutiful servants, "bootblacks, and hotel waiters, grinning from ear to ear and bowing and curtseying for the extra tips," *A Voice from the South* (1892; reprint, New York: Oxford University Press, 1988), 206. A reviewer for the *Critic* struck a similar note, attributing the failure of *An Imperative*

Duty to Howells's "ignorance of the race," adding that the author "likes the race . . . as the Princess Napraxine likes the wolves in Russia—in theory and at a distance." See Martha Banta's "Introduction" to *The Shadow of a Dream and An Imperative Duty,* ed. David J. Nordloh et al. (Bloomington: Indiana University Press, 1970), ix. More recently, Houston Baker has commented on Howells's "myopia" in dealing with issues of race, and Kenneth Warren has written with great insight on the politics of racial representation in Howellsian realism. See Baker, *The Workings of the Spirit: The Poetics of Afro-American Women's Writing* (Chicago: University of Chicago Press, 1991), 34; and Warren, *Black and White Strangers: Race and American Literary Realism* (Chicago: University of Chicago Press, 1993), 65–66.

27. Howells's "Mrs. Johnson" first appeared in the *Atlantic Monthly* in 1868 and was later included in *Suburban Sketches.* Subsequent references to the 1872 James R. Osgood edition are provided in the text.

28. This formulation is indebted to Amy Kaplan's discussion of the many layered concept of "common ground" in Howells's thinking about realism and social change. She explains that, rather than "jar readers with the shock of otherness," realism works "to insure that social difference can be transcended in the medium of the commonplace. Howells thus envisioned realism as a strategy for containing social difference and controlling social conflict within a cohesive common ground." See *The Social Construction of American Realism* (Chicago: University of Chicago Press, 1988), 23.

29. Howells, "An East-Side Ramble," in *Impressions and Experiences* (New York: Harper, 1896), 144.

30. Howells, *The Shadow of a Dream and An Imperative Duty,* ed. David J. Nordloh et al. (Bloomington: Indiana University Press, 1970), 3. Subsequent references appear in the text.

31. This quotation appears in the serial edition of *An Imperative Duty* (*Harper's Monthly* 83 (July 1891): 191), which was criticized for its demeaning characterization of the Irish. Howells objected that Olney's perspective should not be confused with his own, but agreed to remove this and other controversial passages for book publication. See Banta's "Introduction" and Jeffrey A. Clymer's discussion in "Race and the Protocol of American Citizenship in William Dean Howells's *An Imperative Duty,*" *American Literary Realism* 30 (Spring 1998): 31–52.

32. Henry James, *The Portrait of a Lady* (1881; reprint, Boston: Houghton Mifflin, 1963), 172. Thomas Peyser creates a particularly compelling image of Howells as a tentative psychologist in "Those Other Selves: Consciousness in the 1890 Publications of Howells and the James Brothers," *American Literary Realism* 25 (Fall 1992): 20–37. See also

Andrew Delbanco, "Howells and the Suppression of Knowledge," *Southern Review* 19 (1983): 765–84.

33. Kaplan, *The Social Construction of American Realism*, 37.

34. Howells, *A Modern Instance* (1882; reprint, New York: Library of America, 1982), 586.

35. For a more detailed account of Rhoda's transformation, see my essay "Writing Realism: Policing Consciousness: Howells and the Black Body," *American Literature* 67 (December 1995): 701–24.

36. Isabel's profound "love" of African Americans expresses itself in a desire to "own them," a fantasy that is curiously shared by the narrator of "Mrs. Johnson," who explains that he and his wife would have chosen, "if we could, to bear a strand of grotesque beads, or a handful of brazen gauds, and traffic them for some sable maid with crisped locks, whom, uncoffing from the captive train beside the desert, we should make to do our general housework forever, through the right of lawful purchase" (*Suburban Sketches*, 18).

This idea is repeated again by Rhoda Aldgate, prior to the revelation of her "savage" ancestry, when she spots a diminutive black waiter and declares: "he's so sweet! I should like to *own* him, and keep him as long as he lived. Isn't it a shame that we can't *buy* them, Dr. Olney, as we used to do?" (*An Imperative Duty,* 39; emphasis in original).

37. Leo Bersani, *A Future for Astyanax: Character and Desire in Literature* (Boston: Little, Brown, 1976), x.

CHAPTER 2

1. Mark Twain, "Three Thousand Years Among the Microbes," in *Mark Twain's Which Was the Dream and Other Symbolic Writings of the Later Years,* ed. John S. Tuckey (Berkeley: University of California Press, 1968), 436. Hereafter cited within the text.

2. William Dean Howells, *Letters Home* (New York: Harper & Brothers, 1903), 11.

3. *Mark Twain-Howells Letters: The Correspondence of Samuel L. Clemens and William D. Howells, 1872–1910,* 2 vols., ed. Henry Nash Smith and William M. Gibson (Cambridge, Mass.: Harvard University Press, 1960), 2: 832.

4. James T. Farrell, "Introduction" to *Artie and Pink Marsh: Two Novels by George Ade* (Chicago: University of Chicago Press, 1963), x–xi.

5. George Ade, *Artie and Pink Marsh: Two Novels by George Ade* (Chicago: University of Chicago Press, 1963), 119, hereafter cited within the text.

6. Some important examples of this view are collected in *Satire or Evasion: Black Perspectives on Huckleberry Finn,* ed. James S. Leonard,

Thomas A. Tenney, and Thadious M. Davis (Durham, N.C.: Duke University Press, 1992).

7. See Ann Charters, *Nobody: The Story of Bert Williams* (Toronto: Macmillan, 1970). Another excellent resource is Leah Kathleen Cothern, "The Coon Song: A Study of American Music, Entertainment, and Racism" (Masters Thesis, University of Oregon, 1990).

8. Arthur Lamb and Bernard Adler, "I Want a Real Coon," Special Collections, University of Oregon.

9. Henry Nash Smith and William M. Gibson offer this suggestion in *Mark Twain-Howells Letters,* 2: 832.

10. Farrell, *Artie and Pink Marsh,* x.

11. Larzer Ziff, *The American 1890s: Life and Times of an American Generation* (New York: Viking, 1966), 158.

12. Farrell, *Artie and Pink Marsh,* x.

13. Mark Twain, *Sketches, New and Old* (1875; reprint, New York: Oxford University Press, 1996), 231–32. Hereafter cited within the text.

14. Peter Stallybrass and Allon White, *The Politics and Poetics of Transgression* (Ithaca, N.Y.: Cornell University Press, 1986), 200.

15. Ibid., 199–200.

16. Ben Jerome and Frank Abbott, "Nothin' But a Coon," Special Collections, University of Oregon.

17. Both Randall Knoper's *Acting Naturally: Mark Twain in the Culture of Performance* (Berkeley: University of California Press, 1995) and Bruce Michelson's *Mark Twain on the Loose: A Comic Writer and the American Self* (Amherst, Mass.: University of Massachusetts Press, 1995) have been indispensable in helping me to understand how Twain employs conventions associated with traditional ethnic burlesque.

18. Mark Twain, *Mark Twain in Eruption,* ed. Bernard DeVoto (New York: Harper, 1922; reprint, New York: Capricorn, 1968), 110. Hereafter cited in the text.

19. Some important recent studies are by Eric Lott, *Love and Theft: Blackface Minstrelsy and the American Working Class* (New York: Oxford University Press, 1993); Dale Cockrell, *Demons of Disorder: Early Blackface Minstrels and Their World* (Cambridge: Cambridge University Press, 1997); and David Roediger, *The Wages of Whiteness: Race and the Making of the American Working Class* (London: Verso, 1991).

20. Howells, *Letters Home,* 111.

21. Lott, *Love and Theft,* 20.

22. Lawrence Levine, *Highbrow/Lowbrow: The Emergence of Cultural Hierarchy in America* (Cambridge, Mass.: Harvard University Press, 1988); David Roediger, *The Wages of Whiteness;* Dale Cockrell, *Demons of Disorder.*

23. Cockrell, *Demons of Disorder*, 58. Hereafter cited in the text.

24. The Virginia Minstrels were pivotal figures in the development of blackface as a form of musical theater after 1840. See Cockrell's insightful discussion of the banjo, whose emergence as a concert instrument corresponds to changes taking place in the structure and reception of minstrel performance during the period (146–55).

25. Cockrell theorizes that the disruptive "noise" of early blackface, a legacy of callithumpian rioting, was supplanted by the minstrelsy's "music" after 1840. In support of that hypothesis, Twain recalled that when minstrelsy arrived in Hannibal, Missouri, the show's musical repertoire included only "rudely comic" songs that were performed in "a very broad negro dialect," such as "Buffalo Gals," "Camptown Races," and "Old Dan Tucker." The "pristine purity" of these early performances underwent an important change with the gradual incorporation of sentimental songs, many with Irish themes, including "Sweet Ellen Bayne," "Nelly Bly," "A Life on the Ocean Wave," and "The Larboard Watch." See *Mark Twain in Eruption*, 114.

26. *Mark Twain in Eruption*, 115–18. Hereafter cited in the text.

27. Pierre Bourdieu, *Distinction: A Social Critique of the Judgment of Taste*, trans. Richard Nice (Cambridge, Mass.: Harvard University Press, 1984), 4.

28. Lott, *Love and Theft*, 142.

29. See T. Jackson Lears, *No Place of Grace: Antimodernism and the Transformation of American Culture, 1880–1920* (New York: Pantheon, 1981), and Tom Lutz, *American Nervousness, 1903: An Anecdotal History* (Ithaca, N.Y.: Cornell University Press, 1991).

30. *Mark Twain in Eruption*, 110.

31. E. W. Kemble, "Illustrating *Huckleberry Finn*," *Colophon* 1 (1930): 44–5.

32. Teona Tome Gneiting discusses Twain's decision to search the "comic papers" in "Picture and Text: A Theory of Illustrated Fiction in the Nineteenth Century" (Ph.D. diss., University of California, Los Angeles, 1977), 197.

33. Earl F. Briden, "Kemble's 'Speciality' and the Pictorial Countertext of *Huckleberry Finn*," *The Mark Twain Journal* 26 (Fall 1988): 2–14.

34. Briden compares these two illustrations (5). Beverly R. David has also written extensively on Twain's relation to Kemble in "The Pictorial *Huck Finn*: Mark Twain and His Illustrator, E. W. Kemble," *American Quarterly* 26 (October 1974) and *Mark Twain and His Illustrators: Volume 1 (1869–1875)* (Troy, N.Y.: Whitson, 1986). More background is available in Allison R. Ensor, "The Illustrating of *Huckleberry Finn*: A Centennial Perspective," in *One Hundred Years of Huckleberry Finn*, ed. Robert Sattelmeyer and J. Donald Crowley (Columbia: University of Missouri Press, 1985).

35. Briden, "Kemble's 'Speciality' and the Pictorial Countertext of Huck-leberry Finn," 5, 12.

36. Guy Cardwell, *The Man Who Was Mark Twain: Images and Ideologies* (New Haven, Conn.: Yale University Press, 1991), 200.

37. Ellen Moers, quoted in Jackson P. Wysong, "Samuel Clemens' Atti-tude toward the Negro as Demonstrated in *Pudd'nhead Wilson* and *A Connecticut Yankee in King Arthur's Court*," *Xavier Studies* 7 (July 1968): 43.

38. Douglass Anderson, "Reading the Pictures in *Huckleberry Finn*," *Ari-zona Quarterly* 42 (Summer 1986): 118–19. See also Kelly Anspaugh, "The Innocent Eye" E. W. Kemble's Illustrations to *Adventures of Huckleberry Finn*," *American Literary Realism* 25 (Winter 1993): 16–30.

39. Fredrick Woodard and Donnarae MacCann, "Minstrel Shackles and Nineteenth-Century 'Liberality' in *Huckleberry Finn*," in *Satire or Evasion*, 141–53.

40. William Dean Howells, *My Mark Twain* (New York: Harper & Broth-ers, 1910).

41. Shelley Fisher Fishkin, *Was Huck Black? Mark Twain and African-American Voices* (New York: Oxford University Press, 1993).

42. See Gneiting, "Picture and Text," 201.

43. See Ralph Ellison, "Change the Joke and Slip the Yoke," *Partisan Review* 25 (Spring 1958): 212–22, and David L. Smith, "Huck, Jim, and American Racial Discourse," in *Satire or Evasion*, 103–123.

44. William Dean Howells, *Selected Literary Criticism, Vol. 2: 1886–1897*, ed. David J. Nordloh et al. (Bloomington: Indiana University Press, 1993), 353–54.

45. This is perhaps an overly complicated way of saying that Twain is fascinated not only with ethnic humor but with the way audiences react to ethnic humor, and that his fascination plays itself out both within the text and in the novel's effort to provoke a particular kind of reaction from *its* readership. In identifying Twain's primary audi-ence as a "readership," I have, of course, already identified an impor-tant paradox, for while *Huckleberry Finn* begs to be received as a kind of burlesque "performance" (note its many set pieces, soliloquies, speeches and plays, as well as Twain's use of the raft as a moveable stage), literary texts by nature compel the passive and private experi-ence that, according to Twain, spells the death of humor. Thus I do not mean to suggest that the novel invites us to become a kind of ideal minstrel audience, a version of the "jaded souls" who rise "in a body" to shake the house with their laughter in response to the Christy Minstrels. Although it is important to recognize that this form of response animates Twain's thinking about the possibilities of literary "performance," I do not believe that in order to be "good" readers of the novel we must aspire to be the sort of readers Twain

envisions (that is, the sort of readers who love ethnic burlesque and respond to it in dynamic ways). This is a delicate and a crucial point: I think we can, as readers, encounter "the full force of Mark Twain's humor," as I have put it above, without becoming irresponsibly complicit in the game Twain is playing. I am less sure that we can avoid this sort of wholesale complicity when we ourselves perform Twain's ethnic comedy in teaching the novel to students.

46. Quotations from the novel in this and subsequent paragraphs are taken from Mark Twain, *Adventures of Huckleberry Finn,* ed. Walter Blair and Victor Fischer (1885; reprint, Berkeley: University of California Press, 1985).

47. Anthony Berret, "*Huckleberry Finn* and the Minstrel Show," *American Studies* 27 (Fall 1986): 37–49.

48. For an example of the debate over this episode, see Fishkin, *Was Huck Black?* (88–9), including her account of Sterling Brown's position in *The Negro in American Fiction* (1935; reprint, Port Washington, N.Y.: Kennikat Press, 1937), 68.

49. I hope I have made my attitude toward this variety of "fun" perfectly clear and that I will not be misunderstood as encouraging readers to rediscover the entertainment value of an unquestionably racist form. In walking this narrow line, I have tried to suggest that we can and should think critically about the meanings of ethnic burlesque in its overlapping graphic, literary, and performative contexts, even if doing so requires a measure of participation in rituals of exclusion and debasement. I recognize the inherent dangers of such participation, especially as they affect the classroom: when are we "understanding" racist humor with appropriate critical detachment, and when are we "enjoying" it? Isn't there "enjoyment" in arriving at critical "understanding," and is this enjoyment really any different from the reaction "coon" comedy was designed to produce in its original audience? Nevertheless, I feel strongly that this risk is worth taking and that we perhaps risk as much or more by omitting these forms of representation from our thinking about American literary culture.

50. Charles W. Chesnutt, *The Conjure Woman and Other Conjure Tales,* ed. Richard H. Brodhead (1899; reprint, Durham, N.C.: Duke University Press, 1993), 172–82. For a discussion of Chesnutt's use of the stereotype, see Eric J. Sundquist, *To Wake the Nations: Race in the Making of American Literature* (Cambridge, Mass.: Harvard University Press, 1993), 380.

51. Mark Twain, *A Connecticut Yankee in King Arthur's Court,* ed. Bernard L. Stein (1889; reprint, Berkeley: University of California Press, 1979), 300.

CHAPTER 3

1. Henry James, *The American Scene* (1907; reprint, Bloomington: Indiana University Press, 1968), 64. Hereafter cited within the text.

2. James, "Preface" to *The Golden Bowl* (New York: Charles Scribner's Sons, 1909) ix. For an interpretation of James's complex relation to graphic art, see Viola Hopkins Winner, *Henry James and the Visual Arts* (Charlottesville: University Press of Virginia, 1970). Teone Tone Gneiting also offers insight into James's fascination with the visual arts in "Picture and Text: A Theory of Illustrated Fiction in the Nineteenth Century" (Ph.D. diss., University of California, Los Angeles, 1977).

3. Mark Seltzer makes a related observation in *Henry James and the Art of Power* (Ithaca, N.Y.: Cornell University Press, 1989) 99.

4. James discusses his early reading of Dickens and Thackeray in *A Small Boy and Others* (New York: Charles Scribner's Sons, 1913), 117–20. The sketches of George Du Maurier and Honore Daumier originally appeared in *Harper's Monthly* 95 (1897): 595–97, and *Century* 39 (September 1890): 402–13, respectively, and are reprinted in *Picture and Text* (New York: Harper, 1893), 33–36, 116–144.

5. James, *Picture and Text*, 15

6. Ross Posnock, "Henry James, Veblen, and Adorno: The Crisis of the Modern Self," *Journal of American Studies* 21.1 (1987): 52.

7. Quoted in Posnock, "Affirming the Alien: The Pragmatist Pluralism of *The American Scene*," in *The Cambridge Companion to Henry James*, ed. Jonathan Freedman (New York: Cambridge University Press, 1998), 232.

8. Peter Conn, *The Divided Mind* (Cambridge: Cambridge University Press, 1983), 44. Gert Buelens summarizes a broad range of critical opinion on *The American Scene* in "Possessing the American Scene: Race and Vulgarity, Seduction and Judgment," in *Enacting History in Henry James: Narrative, Power, and Ethics*, ed. Gert Buelens (Cambridge: Cambridge University Press, 1997), 166–92.

9. Posnock, *The Trial of Curiosity: Henry James, William James, and the Challenge of Modernity* (New York: Oxford University Press, 1991), 148.

10. Kenneth Warren, *Black and White Strangers: Race and American Literary Realism* (Chicago: University of Chicago Press, 1993), 114–16. See also the debate on race in *The Henry James Review* 16 (1995): 249–303.

11. Thomas Peyser, *Utopia and Cosmopolis: Globalization in the Era of American Literary Realism* (Durham, N.C.: Duke University Press, 1998), 140.

12. Quoted in Martha Banta, *Barbarous Intercourse: Caricature and the*

Culture of Conduct, 1841–1936 (Chicago: University of Chicago Press, 2003), 176.

13. Ibid.
14. Ibid., 177.
15. Ibid.
16. See Sara Blair, *Henry James and the Writing of Race and Nation* (New York: Cambridge University Press, 1996), especially chapter three, "'Trying to be Natural': Authorship and the Power of Type in *The Princess Casamassima*," and chapter 4, "James, Jack the Ripper, and the Cosmopolitan Jew: Staging Authorship in *The Tragic Muse*."
17. James, *The Golden Bowl*, 2 vols. (New York: Charles Scribner's Sons, 1909), 1:16. Hereafter cited within the text.
18. The concept of "reversion to type" is a common feature of the "scientific" discourse of the period and a frequent event in naturalist fiction. For an interesting reading of the ideological implications of "reversion" theory, see June Howard, *Form and History in American Naturalism* (Chapel Hill: University of North Carolina Press, 1985).
19. James, *Italian Hours* (London: William Heinemann, 1909), 17.
20. Jonathan Freedman, *The Temple of Culture: Assimilation and Anti-Semitism in Literary Anglo-America* (New York: Oxford University Press, 2000), 136.
21. Peyser, *Utopia and Cosmopolis*, 159.
22. Seltzer, *Henry James and the Art of Power*, 71.
23. Freedman, *The Temple of Culture*, 137.
24. Ibid.
25. Peyser, *Utopia and Cosmopolis*, 158.
26. Freedman, *The Temple of Culture*, 146.
27. Ibid.
28. Theodore Adorno, *Negative Dialectics*, trans. E. B. Ashton (1973; reprint, London: Routledge, 1990), 216.
29. See Freedman's chapter on "The Poetics of Cultural Decline: Degeneracy, Assimilation, and the Jew in *The Golden Bowl*," *The Temple of Culture*, 132–48.
30. Posnock describes James's identification with the figure of the Jew in "Henry James, Veblen, and Adorno," 44–5, 49–50.
31. James, *The American Scene*, 138.
32. Peyser, *Utopia and Cosmopolis*, 140.

CHAPTER 4

1. Bentley, "Hunting for the Real," 49.
2. Edith Wharton, *The House of Mirth* (1905; reprint, New York: Bedford, 1994), 159. Hereafter cited in the text.

3. For a contemporary account of the Astor Four Hundred and New York social life generally, see Ralph Pulizer, *New York Society of Parade* (New York: Harper & Brothers, 1910).

4. This phrase appears in the popular song "Nothin' But a Coon" (1901) by Ben Jerome and Frank Abbott. Special Sheet Music Collection, University of Oregon.

5. John J. Appel, "Jews in American Caricature: 1820–1914," *Jewish American History* 71 (September 1981): 112–13.

6. The exchange between *Puck* and the *Jewish Messenger* took place in December 1881, and is reproduced in Appel, 122.

7. Henry James, *The American Scene* (1907; reprint, Bloomington: Indiana University Press, 1968), 1.

8. Mark Twain, *Mark Twain in Eruption,* ed. Bernard DeVoto (New York: Harper & Brothers, 1940), 115.

9. See Beverly R. David, "The Pictorial *Huck Finn:* Mark Twain and His Illustrator, E. W. Kemble," *American Quarterly* 26 (October 1974): 331–51.

10. Appel's "Jews in American Caricature: 1820–1914" is a rich source of material on humor of this variety. See also Jonathan Freedman, *The Temple of Culture: Assimilation and Anti-Semitism in Literary Anglo-America* (New York: Oxford University Press, 2000).

11. David Herman, "Economies of Essence in *The House of Mirth,*" *Edith Wharton Review* 16 (Spring 1999): 7.

12. Jennie A. Kassanoff, "Extinction, Taxidermy, Tableaux Vivants: Staging Race and Class in *The House of Mirth,*" *PMLA* 115 (January 2000): 61.

13. James, *The American Scene,* 132.

14. See Thorstein Veblen, *The Theory of the Leisure Class: An Economic Study of Institutions* (1899; reprint, New York: Mentor, 1955), especially the chapters on "Conspicuous Leisure" and "Conspicuous Consumption." See also Ross Posnock, "Henry James, Veblen and Adorno: The Crisis of the Modern Self," *Journal of American Studies* 21 (Spring 1987): 31–54.

15. *Life* 55 (April 1910).

16. William E. Moddelmog, "Disavowing 'Personality': Privacy and Subjectivity in *The House of Mirth,*" *American Literature* 70 (June 1998): 337–63.

17. Pamela Knights, "Forms of Disembodiment: The Social Subject in *The Age of Innocence,*" in *The Cambridge Companion to Edith Wharton,* ed. Millicent Bell (New York: Cambridge University Press, 1995), 21.

18. Amy Kaplan, *The Social Construction of American Realism* (Chicago: University of Chicago Press, 1988), 65–87.

19. Wharton, *The Custom of the Country* (New York: Charles Scribner's Sons, 1913), 19.

20. For an account of "the inviolate self," see Louis A. Sass, "The Self and Its Vicissitudes in the Psycho-Analytic Avant Garde," in *Constructions of the Self,* ed. George Levine (New Brunswick, N.J.: Rutgers University Press, 1992), 17–58. I also have in mind here a conception of selfhood that gave birth to the language of privacy rights toward the end of the nineteenth century. Moddelmog describes this structure of self as based on "a conception whose emphasis on self-ownership and autonomy comes dangerously close to affirming a kind of radical subjectivism, yet whose rationalist assumptions presuppose the universal nature of truth and knowledge" ("Disavowing 'Personality,'" 338).

21. Eric Lott discusses the dance career of William Henry Lane ("Juba") in *Love and Theft: Blackface Minstrelsy and the American Working Class* (New York: Oxford University Press, 1993), 113–16.

22. See John Barrell, "Sir Joshua Reynolds and the Englishness of English Art," *Nation and Narration,* ed. Homi Bhabha (New York: Routledge, 1990), 154–76.

CHAPTER 5

1. Chesnutt described himself as "an American of acknowledged African descent" in his initial correspondence with Houghton Mifflin in 1891, though his ethnicity did not become widely known among readers until 1899. See *"To Be an Author": Letters of Charles W. Chesnutt,* ed. Joseph R. McElrath and Robert C. Leitz III, (Princeton, N.J.: Princeton University Press, 1997), 75–76. Also Helen M. Chesnutt, *Charles Waddell Chesnutt: Pioneer of the Color Line* (Chapel Hill: University of North Carolina Press, 1952), 68–69.

2. Henry James, *The American Scene* (1907; reprint, Bloomington: Indiana University Press, 1968), 308–9.

3. Ernest Hogan, "All Coons Look Alike to Me" (1896), Special Sheet Music Collection, University of Oregon.

4. Charles Johanningsmeier takes the unusual step of discussing the significance of Chesnutt's early sketches in "What We Can Learn from a Better Bibliographical Record of Charles W. Chesnutt's Periodical Fiction," *North Carolina Literary Review* 8 (1999): 84–96.

5. William L. Andrews, *The Literary Career of Charles W. Chesnutt* (Baton Rouge: Louisiana State University Press, 1980), 18.

6. Charles W. Chesnutt, "Race Prejudice: Its Causes and Cures," a speech delivered to the Boston Literary and Historical Society, June 25, 1905, reprinted in *Charles W. Chesnutt: Essays and Speeches,* eds. Joseph R. McElrath, Jr., Robert C. Leitz III, and Jesse S. Crisler (Stanford, Calif.: Stanford University Press, 1999), 232.

7. Chesnutt, "Race Prejudice," *Essays and Speeches,* 215.

8. Ibid., 234.

9. Charles W. Chesnutt, "What Is a White Man?," *The Independent,* May 30, 1889, reprinted in *Essays and Speeches,* 68.

10. Charles W. Chesnutt, "The Future American: What the Race Is Likely to Become in the Process of Time," *Boston Evening Transcript,* August 18, 1900, reprinted in *Essays and Speeches,* 121-25. Hereafter cited within the text.

11. Charles W. Chesnutt, "A Fatal Restriction," *Puck* (May 1, 1889): 166.

12. "Dave's Neckliss" appeared originally in *The Atlantic Monthly* 64 (October 1889): 500-508. The story is reprinted in Charles W. Chesnutt, *The Conjure Woman and Other Conjure Tales,* ed. Richard H. Brodhead (Durham, N.C.: Duke University Press, 1993), 107. References to this edition appear within the text.

13. Charles W. Chesnutt to Albion Tourgee, September 26, 1889, reprinted in *"To Be an Author": Letters of Charles W. Chesnutt,* 44-46.

14. Eric Sundquist, *To Wake the Nations: Race in the Making of American Literature* (Cambridge, Mass.: Harvard University Press, 1993), 382.

15. John describes "the Oriental cast of the negro's imagination" in "Po' Sandy," which first appeared in *The Atlantic Monthly* 61 (May 1888): 605-11, reprinted in *The Conjure Woman and Other Conjure Tales,* 46. Referring to this exotic and endearing quality of Julius's conjure tales, Frances Richardson Keller (*An American Crusade: The Life of Charles Waddell Chesnutt* [Provo, Utah: Brigham Young University Press, 1978]) observes that "Dave's Neckliss" bears more in common with Kafka's nightmarish "The Metamorphosis" than with Joel Chandler Harris's Uncle Remus tales (141).

16. Chesnutt, *The Conjure Woman and Other Conjure Tales,* 55.

17. Ibid., 172.

18. Sundquist, *To Wake the Nations,* 381.

19. Chesnutt, *The Conjure Woman and Other Conjure Tales,* 55.

20. "A Victim of Heredity; or, Why the Darkey Loves Chicken" first appeared in *Self-Culture Magazine* 11 (July (1900): 404-409, reprinted in *The Conjure Woman and Other Conjure Tales.* This edition is cited within the text.

21. Sundquist, *To Wake the Nations,* 380.

22. Amiri Baraka (Leroi Jones), *Blues People: Negro Music in White America* (New York: William Morrow, 1963), 58-59.

23. *The Journals of Charles W. Chesnutt,* ed. Richard Brodhead (Durham, N.C.: Duke University Press, 1993), 139.

24. Chesnutt to Albion Tourgee, September 26, 1889, reprinted in *"To Be an Author": Letters of Charles W. Chesnutt,* 44.

25. *The Conjure Woman and Other Conjure Tales,* 185. "The Wife of His Youth" first appeared in *The Atlantic Monthly* 82 (July 1898): 55-61, reprinted in *The Wife of His Youth and Other Stories of the Color Line*

(Ann Arbor: University of Michigan Press, 1968). References to this edition appear within the text.

26. Werner Sollers, *Beyond Ethnicity: Consent and Descent in American Culture* (New York: Oxford University Press, 1986), 159–60.

27. Abraham Cahan, *Yekl and the Imported Bridegroom and Other Stories of Yiddish New York* (New York: Dover, 1970), 34.

28. William Dean Howells, "Mr. Charles W. Chesnutt's Stories," *Atlantic Monthly* 85 (May 1900): 699–701, reprinted in *Critical Essays on Charles Chesnutt*, ed. Joseph R. McElrath, Jr. (New York: G. K. Hall, 1999), 52–54. This edition is hereafter cited in the text. Howells discussed Chesnutt's fiction in another important review, "A Psychological Counter-Current in Recent Fiction," *North American Review* 173 (1901): 872–88. For a thorough account of the brief Howells/Chesnutt correspondence, see Joseph R. McElrath, Jr., "W. D. Howells and Race: Charles W. Chesnutt's Disappointment of the Dean," *Nineteenth-Century Literature* 51 (March 1997): 474–99.

29. William Dean Howells, "Concerning a Council of Imperfection," *Literature* 1 (April 7, 1899): 290.

30. Howells, "Concerning a Council of Imperfection," 290.

31. Ibid.

32. William Dean Howells, "Paul Laurence Dunbar," in *William Dean Howells: Selected Literary Criticism, Vol. 2: 1886–1897,* ed. David J. Nordloh, et al. (Bloomington: Indiana University Press, 1993), 280. Hereafter cited in the text.

33. Joseph R. McElrath, Jr. comes at this question from a different direction but reaches a similar conclusion in the aptly entitled essay, "Why Charles Chesnutt Is Not a Realist," *American Literary Realism* 32 (Winter 2000): 91–108. See also William L. Andrews, "William Dean Howells and Charles W. Chesnutt: Criticism and Race Fiction in the Age of Booker T. Washington," *American Literature* 48 (1976): 327–39.

INDEX

Ade, George
  Pink Marsh, 71–78, 79, 83
Adorno, Theodore, 124
advertising, 20
Alden, Henry Mills, 20
Aldrich, Thomas Bailey, 20
Anderson, Douglass, 91
Andrews, William, 152–53
anti-Semitism, 17, 28–31, 102, 105–6,
  125, 129–37
Appel, John, 129–30
Astor, Caroline Jacob, 127
Astor Four Hundred, The, 127
Atlantic Monthly, 5, 14, 20, 152,
  170
Auerbach, Erich, 5–6

Balzac, Honoré de, 9–10, 41–43, 46,
  68
Banta, Martha, 113–15, 118
Baraka, Amiri [Leroi Jones], 164
Barnum, P. T., 24
Bentley, Nancy, 127
Berret, Anthony, 94
Bersani, Leo, 67–68
blackface. *See* minstrelsy
Bourdieu, Pierre, 87
Bourne, Randolph, 38
Boyeson, Hjalmar Hjorth, 171
Briden, Earl, 89–91
le Brun, Charles, 13

Cahan, Abraham, 171
  Yekl: A Tale of the New York Ghetto,
  167–68
Cardwell, Guy, 91
caricature
  of African Americans, 26–28,
    173n.1, 177n.61. *See also* Kemble,
    minstrelsy, "real coon"
  in American fiction, 35–40, 59–61,
    137–38, 169–72
  of Asians, 78–81
  contrasted with "realism," 3–9
  as a dimension of "realist" aesthet-
    ics, 9–10
  of Eastern Europeans, 31, 69–71
  of Germans, 31, 49, 58–59,
    180n.15
  of the Irish, 31, 52–54, 61–62,
    177n.56
  of Jews, 28–31, 178n.62. *See also*
    anti-Semitism
  in the "literary" magazines, 16–18
  of Native Americans, 31, 107
  and phrenology, 11–14
  and political satire, 24–25
  as reflexive satire, 32–35, 106–12,
    127–33
  in the weekly papers, 22–31
  of women, 141–46
Carracci, Annibale, 9–10
Cather, Willa, 39